# TEACHER'S PET PUBLICATIONS

## PUZZLE PACK
for
The Things They Carried

based on the book by
Tim O' Brien

Written by
Mary B. Collins

© 2007 Teacher's Pet Publications
All Rights Reserved

The materials in this packet are copyrighted
by Teacher's Pet Publications, Inc.

These pages may be duplicated by the purchaser
for use in the purchaser's own classroom.

Copying any of these materials and distributing them
for any other purpose is a violation of the copyright laws.

© 2007 Teacher's Pet Publications, Inc.
www.tpet.com

## INTRODUCTION
If you already own the LitPlan for this title, this Puzzle Pack will refresh your Unit Resource Materials and Vocabulary Resource Materials sections plus give you additional materials you can substitute into the tests.If you do not already have a complete LitPlan, these pages will give you some supplemental materials to use with your own plan. There are two main groups of materials: one set for unit words (such as characters' names, symbols, places, etc.) and one set for vocabulary words associated with the book.

## WORD LIST
There is a word list for both the unit words and the vocabulary words. These lists show you which words are being used in the materials and the clues or definitions being used for those words. You may want to give students a word list with clues/definitions to help them, or you may want students to only have a word list (without clues/definitions) if you want them to work a little harder. Both are available for duplication. The word lists can also be your "calling key" for the bingo games.

## FILL IN THE BLANK AND MATCHING
There are 4 each of the fill in the blank and matching worksheets for both the unit and vocabulary words. These pages can be used either as extra worksheets for students or as objective parts of a unit test. They can be done individually if students need extra help or as a whole class activity to review the material covered.

## MAGIC SQUARES
The magic squares not only reinforce the material covered but also work on reasoning and math skills. Many teachers have told us that their students really enjoy doing these!

## WORD SEARCH PUZZLES
The word search words go in all directions, as indicated on your answer keys. Two of the word search puzzles have the clues listed rather than the words. This makes the puzzle a little more difficult, but it reinforces the material better. Two word search puzzles have words only for students who find the clue puzzles too difficult.

## CROSSWORD PUZZLES
Both unit and vocabulary word sections have 4 crossword puzzles.

## BINGO CARDS
There are 32 individual bingo cards for the unit words and 32 individual bingo cards for the vocabulary words. You can use your word list as a "call list," calling the words at random and marking them off of your list as you go, or you could use the flash cards by cutting them apart and drawing the words at random from a hat (or box or whatever). To make a better review, you might ask for the definition and spelling of each word as you call it out–or you could call out the definitions and have students tell you the words they need to look for on the puzzle.

## JUGGLE LETTERS
The vocabulary juggle letter game is intended to help students learn the spellings of the words. One sheet has the definitions listed on it as an extra help for students who need it or to reinforce the definitions if you choose to do so.

## FLASH CARDS
We've included a set of vocabulary flash cards you can duplicate, cut, and fold for your students. Some teachers make a few sets for general use by the class; others make a set for each student. Some teachers duplicate them for each student and have the students cut & fold their own. You can cut out just the words and put them in a hat, have each student pick out one word and write the definition and a sentence for that word. Students then swap words and papers, with the next student adding a sentence of his own under the last one. You can have students swap as many times as you like. Each time the student will read the sentences written prior to his own and then add a sentence. You can cut out the words and definitions separately and play "I Have; Who Has?" Each student in the room draws a word and definition. The first student says, "I have (the name of the word). Who has the definition?" The student with the definition reads it then says, "I have (the name of the vocabulary word she has). Who has the definition?" The round continues until all words and definitions have been given.

**The Things They Carried Word List**

| No. | Word | Clue/Definition |
|---|---|---|
| 1. | ALPHA | Name of the Company |
| 2. | AZAR | Aids O'Brien in getting revenge |
| 3. | BERDAHL | Hero of the narrator's life |
| 4. | BOWKER | Commits suicide |
| 5. | BUFFALO | Water ___ was killed because of Rat's grief |
| 6. | CANADA | Place many draft-dodgers fled to |
| 7. | CARRIED | The Things They ___ |
| 8. | CHURCHES | Kiowa advised soldiers not to damage or profane these. |
| 9. | CORPSE | Narrator refused to shake hands with one |
| 10. | COURAGE | Norman asked the narrator to write Speaking Of ___. |
| 11. | DANCING | Azar mocked this. |
| 12. | DECLOTTER | O'Brien's summer job in 1968 |
| 13. | ENGAGED | Mark compromised with Mary Anne and they became ___. |
| 14. | EVIL | Narrator found it difficult to admit he was capable of this. |
| 15. | EXCREMENT | The muddy field was full of this. |
| 16. | FOOT | Kiley shot himself there. |
| 17. | FOSSE | Brought his girlfriend to Vietnam for a visit |
| 18. | FUND | Note with money in envelope said Emergency ___. |
| 19. | GREEN | The ___ Berets used the compound as their base. |
| 20. | GRUNT | Any soldier |
| 21. | HENRY | His girlfriend dumped him in October; monks liked him |
| 22. | HUMP | To carry |
| 23. | IRONIC | Azar thought it was ___ to die in a field of excrement. |
| 24. | JACKKNIFE | Object of Strunk and Jensen's fistfight |
| 25. | JUNGLE | Mary Anne disappears into the ___. |
| 26. | KATHLEEN | O'Brien's daughter |
| 27. | KIOWA | Native American soldier |
| 28. | LAKE | Norman drove around it. |
| 29. | LAVENDER | Jimmy Cross never forgave himself for this soldier's death. |
| 30. | LEMON | Fainted during a dentist visit |
| 31. | LINDA | Fourth-grade girlfriend of O'Brien |
| 32. | LODGE | Narrator drove to the Tip Top ___ |
| 33. | MARTHA | Lt. Cross burned her picture |
| 34. | MEDIC | Jorgenson's job |
| 35. | MOCCASINS | Kiowa's were in the rucksack. |
| 36. | NEW | Kiowa received an illustrated ___ Testament. |
| 37. | NOSE | Jensen broke his own |
| 38. | OBRIEN | Believes that stories can save lives |
| 39. | PANTYHOSE | Good-luck item for Dobbins |
| 40. | PATROL | The listening ___ heard sounds foreign to the jungle. |
| 41. | PHOTO | It indirectly causes Kiowa's death. |
| 42. | PISTOL | Object that broke Jensen's nose |
| 43. | RAT | Known for exaggerating |
| 44. | SANDERS | Confessed he made up parts of the story |
| 45. | SANK | Kiowa ___ into the mud. |
| 46. | SILVER | Norman didn't win the ___ Star. |
| 47. | SISTER | Rat wrote to Curt Lemon's |
| 48. | SPOOKED | To get killed |
| 49. | STAR | Shape of the Vietnamese soldier's wound |
| 50. | STORIES | Tim tries to save Timmy's life using these. |
| 51. | SWEETHEART | Mary Anne was the ___ of the Song Tra Bong. |

## The Things They Carried Word List Continued

| No. | Word | Clue/Definition |
|---|---|---|
| 52. | TED | Escapes the realities of the war by using drugs |
| 53. | TRIP | Narrator gave Kathleen a ___ to Vietnam as a present. |
| 54. | TRUE | A war story is ___ if it embarrasses the listener. |
| 55. | TUMOR | Cause of Linda's demise |
| 56. | VIETNAM | Country & name of the war |
| 57. | WELL | Dobbins threatens to put Azar in one. |

The Things They Carried Fill In The Blanks 1

_____  1. Brought his girlfriend to Vietnam for a visit

_____  2. Azar mocked this.

_____  3. O'Brien's summer job in 1968

_____  4. Any soldier

_____  5. It indirectly causes Kiowa's death.

_____  6. Water ____ was killed because of Rat's grief

_____  7. To get killed

_____  8. Jimmy Cross never forgave himself for this soldier's death.

_____  9. Hero of the narrator's life

_____  10. Mary Anne was the ____ of the Song Tra Bong.

_____  11. A war story is ____ if it embarrasses the listener.

_____  12. To carry

_____  13. Kiley shot himself there.

_____  14. Kiowa received an illustrated ____ Testament.

_____  15. The Things They ____

_____  16. Narrator found it difficult to admit he was capable of this.

_____  17. Lt. Cross burned her picture

_____  18. Good-luck item for Dobbins

_____  19. Norman drove around it.

_____  20. Kiowa advised soldiers not to damage or profane these.

The Things They Carried Fill In The Blanks 1 Answer Key

| | |
|---|---|
| FOSSE | 1. Brought his girlfriend to Vietnam for a visit |
| DANCING | 2. Azar mocked this. |
| DECLOTTER | 3. O'Brien's summer job in 1968 |
| GRUNT | 4. Any soldier |
| PHOTO | 5. It indirectly causes Kiowa's death. |
| BUFFALO | 6. Water ___ was killed because of Rat's grief |
| SPOOKED | 7. To get killed |
| LAVENDER | 8. Jimmy Cross never forgave himself for this soldier's death. |
| BERDAHL | 9. Hero of the narrator's life |
| SWEETHEART | 10. Mary Anne was the ___ of the Song Tra Bong. |
| TRUE | 11. A war story is ___ if it embarrasses the listener. |
| HUMP | 12. To carry |
| FOOT | 13. Kiley shot himself there. |
| NEW | 14. Kiowa received an illustrated ___ Testament. |
| CARRIED | 15. The Things They ___ |
| EVIL | 16. Narrator found it difficult to admit he was capable of this. |
| MARTHA | 17. Lt. Cross burned her picture |
| PANTYHOSE | 18. Good-luck item for Dobbins |
| LAKE | 19. Norman drove around it. |
| CHURCHES | 20. Kiowa advised soldiers not to damage or profane these. |

The Things They Carried Fill In The Blanks 2

1. The ___ Berets used the compound as their base.
2. Kiley shot himself there.
3. To get killed
4. Country & name of the war
5. Object of Strunk and Jensen's fistfight
6. Hero of the narrator's life
7. Native American soldier
8. Jensen broke his own
9. Norman drove around it.
10. Azar thought it was ___ to die in a field of excrement.
11. Kiowa advised soldiers not to damage or profane these.
12. Azar mocked this.
13. Narrator gave Kathleen a ___ to Vietnam as a present.
14. Object that broke Jensen's nose
15. O'Brien's summer job in 1968
16. Kiowa's were in the rucksack.
17. Aids O'Brien in getting revenge
18. His girlfriend dumped him in October; monks liked him
19. Kiowa ___ into the mud.
20. Shape of the Vietnamese soldier's wound

The Things They Carried Fill In The Blanks 2 Answer Key

| | |
|---|---|
| GREEN | 1. The ___ Berets used the compound as their base. |
| FOOT | 2. Kiley shot himself there. |
| SPOOKED | 3. To get killed |
| VIETNAM | 4. Country & name of the war |
| JACKKNIFE | 5. Object of Strunk and Jensen's fistfight |
| BERDAHL | 6. Hero of the narrator's life |
| KIOWA | 7. Native American soldier |
| NOSE | 8. Jensen broke his own |
| LAKE | 9. Norman drove around it. |
| IRONIC | 10. Azar thought it was ___ to die in a field of excrement. |
| CHURCHES | 11. Kiowa advised soldiers not to damage or profane these. |
| DANCING | 12. Azar mocked this. |
| TRIP | 13. Narrator gave Kathleen a ___ to Vietnam as a present. |
| PISTOL | 14. Object that broke Jensen's nose |
| DECLOTTER | 15. O'Brien's summer job in 1968 |
| MOCCASINS | 16. Kiowa's were in the rucksack. |
| AZAR | 17. Aids O'Brien in getting revenge |
| HENRY | 18. His girlfriend dumped him in October; monks liked him |
| SANK | 19. Kiowa ___ into the mud. |
| STAR | 20. Shape of the Vietnamese soldier's wound |

The Things They Carried Fill In The Blanks 3

1. The Things They ___
2. Hero of the narrator's life
3. Shape of the Vietnamese soldier's wound
4. Jorgenson's job
5. Narrator gave Kathleen a ___ to Vietnam as a present.
6. Mark compromised with Mary Anne and they became ___.
7. Kiowa advised soldiers not to damage or profane these.
8. Norman drove around it.
9. Kiowa's were in the rucksack.
10. Escapes the realities of the war by using drugs
11. Azar thought it was ___ to die in a field of excrement.
12. The ___ Berets used the compound as their base.
13. It indirectly causes Kiowa's death.
14. O'Brien's daughter
15. A war story is ____ if it embarrasses the listener.
16. Mary Anne was the ___ of the Song Tra Bong.
17. Lt. Cross burned her picture
18. To get killed
19. Country & name of the war
20. Object of Strunk and Jensen's fistfight

The Things They Carried Fill In The Blanks 3 Answer Key

| | |
|---|---|
| CARRIED | 1. The Things They ___ |
| BERDAHL | 2. Hero of the narrator's life |
| STAR | 3. Shape of the Vietnamese soldier's wound |
| MEDIC | 4. Jorgenson's job |
| TRIP | 5. Narrator gave Kathleen a ___ to Vietnam as a present. |
| ENGAGED | 6. Mark compromised with Mary Anne and they became ___. |
| CHURCHES | 7. Kiowa advised soldiers not to damage or profane these. |
| LAKE | 8. Norman drove around it. |
| MOCCASINS | 9. Kiowa's were in the rucksack. |
| TED | 10. Escapes the realities of the war by using drugs |
| IRONIC | 11. Azar thought it was ___ to die in a field of excrement. |
| GREEN | 12. The ___ Berets used the compound as their base. |
| PHOTO | 13. It indirectly causes Kiowa's death. |
| KATHLEEN | 14. O'Brien's daughter |
| TRUE | 15. A war story is ___ if it embarrasses the listener. |
| SWEETHEART | 16. Mary Anne was the ___ of the Song Tra Bong. |
| MARTHA | 17. Lt. Cross burned her picture |
| SPOOKED | 18. To get killed |
| VIETNAM | 19. Country & name of the war |
| JACKKNIFE | 20. Object of Strunk and Jensen's fistfight |

The Things They Carried Fill In The Blanks 4

1. Believes that stories can save lives
2. Mark compromised with Mary Anne and they became ___.
3. A war story is ___ if it embarrasses the listener.
4. Brought his girlfriend to Vietnam for a visit
5. Tim tries to save Timmy's life using these.
6. O'Brien's summer job in 1968
7. Mary Anne disappears into the ___.
8. The muddy field was full of this.
9. Confessed he made up parts of the story
10. Lt. Cross burned her picture
11. Cause of Linda's demise
12. Narrator drove to the Tip Top ___
13. To get killed
14. Water ___ was killed because of Rat's grief
15. Narrator refused to shake hands with one
16. Object of Strunk and Jensen's fistfight
17. Escapes the realities of the war by using drugs
18. Jensen broke his own
19. Aids O'Brien in getting revenge
20. Jorgenson's job

The Things They Carried Fill In The Blanks 4 Answer Key

| | | |
|---|---|---|
| OBRIEN | 1. | Believes that stories can save lives |
| ENGAGED | 2. | Mark compromised with Mary Anne and they became ___. |
| TRUE | 3. | A war story is ___ if it embarrasses the listener. |
| FOSSE | 4. | Brought his girlfriend to Vietnam for a visit |
| STORIES | 5. | Tim tries to save Timmy's life using these. |
| DECLOTTER | 6. | O'Brien's summer job in 1968 |
| JUNGLE | 7. | Mary Anne disappears into the ___. |
| EXCREMENT | 8. | The muddy field was full of this. |
| SANDERS | 9. | Confessed he made up parts of the story |
| MARTHA | 10. | Lt. Cross burned her picture |
| TUMOR | 11. | Cause of Linda's demise |
| LODGE | 12. | Narrator drove to the Tip Top ___ |
| SPOOKED | 13. | To get killed |
| BUFFALO | 14. | Water ___ was killed because of Rat's grief |
| CORPSE | 15. | Narrator refused to shake hands with one |
| JACKKNIFE | 16. | Object of Strunk and Jensen's fistfight |
| TED | 17. | Escapes the realities of the war by using drugs |
| NOSE | 18. | Jensen broke his own |
| AZAR | 19. | Aids O'Brien in getting revenge |
| MEDIC | 20. | Jorgenson's job |

The Things They Carried Matching 1

___ 1. TRUE         A. Jimmy Cross never forgave himself for this soldier's death.
___ 2. SANDERS      B. Known for exaggerating
___ 3. KIOWA        C. To carry
___ 4. RAT          D. Aids O'Brien in getting revenge
___ 5. BOWKER       E. Water ___ was killed because of Rat's grief
___ 6. OBRIEN       F. Norman drove around it.
___ 7. CANADA       G. Good-luck item for Dobbins
___ 8. TED          H. Rat wrote to Curt Lemon's
___ 9. LINDA        I. Object that broke Jensen's nose
___10. ALPHA        J. The Things They ___
___11. CORPSE       K. Azar thought it was ___ to die in a field of excrement.
___12. IRONIC       L. Escapes the realities of the war by using drugs
___13. PHOTO        M. Fourth-grade girlfriend of O'Brien
___14. HUMP         N. Mary Anne disappears into the ___.
___15. LAKE         O. Name of the Company
___16. SISTER       P. A war story is ____ if it embarrasses the listener.
___17. PISTOL       Q. Confessed he made up parts of the story
___18. PANTYHOSE    R. To get killed
___19. STORIES      S. Tim tries to save Timmy's life using these.
___20. CARRIED      T. Believes that stories can save lives
___21. BUFFALO      U. Native American soldier
___22. AZAR         V. Narrator refused to shake hands with one
___23. SPOOKED      W. Place many draft-dodgers fled to
___24. JUNGLE       X. It indirectly causes Kiowa's death.
___25. LAVENDER     Y. Commits suicide

The Things They Carried Matching 1 Answer Key

| | | | |
|---|---|---|---|
| P - 1. | TRUE | A. | Jimmy Cross never forgave himself for this soldier's death. |
| Q - 2. | SANDERS | B. | Known for exaggerating |
| U - 3. | KIOWA | C. | To carry |
| B - 4. | RAT | D. | Aids O'Brien in getting revenge |
| Y - 5. | BOWKER | E. | Water ___ was killed because of Rat's grief |
| T - 6. | OBRIEN | F. | Norman drove around it. |
| W - 7. | CANADA | G. | Good-luck item for Dobbins |
| L - 8. | TED | H. | Rat wrote to Curt Lemon's |
| M - 9. | LINDA | I. | Object that broke Jensen's nose |
| O - 10. | ALPHA | J. | The Things They ___ |
| V - 11. | CORPSE | K. | Azar thought it was ___ to die in a field of excrement. |
| K - 12. | IRONIC | L. | Escapes the realities of the war by using drugs |
| X - 13. | PHOTO | M. | Fourth-grade girlfriend of O'Brien |
| C - 14. | HUMP | N. | Mary Anne disappears into the ___. |
| F - 15. | LAKE | O. | Name of the Company |
| H - 16. | SISTER | P. | A war story is ___ if it embarrasses the listener. |
| I - 17. | PISTOL | Q. | Confessed he made up parts of the story |
| G - 18. | PANTYHOSE | R. | To get killed |
| S - 19. | STORIES | S. | Tim tries to save Timmy's life using these. |
| J - 20. | CARRIED | T. | Believes that stories can save lives |
| E - 21. | BUFFALO | U. | Native American soldier |
| D - 22. | AZAR | V. | Narrator refused to shake hands with one |
| R - 23. | SPOOKED | W. | Place many draft-dodgers fled to |
| N - 24. | JUNGLE | X. | It indirectly causes Kiowa's death. |
| A - 25. | LAVENDER | Y. | Commits suicide |

The Things They Carried Matching 2

___ 1. DANCING  A. Good-luck item for Dobbins
___ 2. LEMON  B. Cause of Linda's demise
___ 3. SILVER  C. Native American soldier
___ 4. PHOTO  D. Shape of the Vietnamese soldier's wound
___ 5. TED  E. The listening ___ heard sounds foreign to the jungle.
___ 6. EVIL  F. It indirectly causes Kiowa's death.
___ 7. KIOWA  G. Norman asked the narrator to write Speaking Of ___.
___ 8. GRUNT  H. A war story is ____ if it embarrasses the listener.
___ 9. GREEN  I. Name of the Company
___10. KATHLEEN  J. The muddy field was full of this.
___11. PANTYHOSE  K. Aids O'Brien in getting revenge
___12. IRONIC  L. Narrator found it difficult to admit he was capable of this.
___13. COURAGE  M. O'Brien's daughter
___14. JACKKNIFE  N. Azar thought it was ___ to die in a field of excrement.
___15. AZAR  O. O'Brien's summer job in 1968
___16. HENRY  P. Fainted during a dentist visit
___17. TRUE  Q. Norman didn't win the ___ Star.
___18. ALPHA  R. Object of Strunk and Jensen's fistfight
___19. EXCREMENT  S. Fourth-grade girlfriend of O'Brien
___20. STAR  T. The ___ Berets used the compound as their base.
___21. TUMOR  U. Any soldier
___22. JUNGLE  V. His girlfriend dumped him in October; monks liked him
___23. DECLOTTER  W. Mary Anne disappears into the ___.
___24. LINDA  X. Azar mocked this.
___25. PATROL  Y. Escapes the realities of the war by using drugs

The Things They Carried Matching 2 Answer Key

| | | | |
|---|---|---|---|
| X - 1. | DANCING | A. | Good-luck item for Dobbins |
| P - 2. | LEMON | B. | Cause of Linda's demise |
| Q - 3. | SILVER | C. | Native American soldier |
| F - 4. | PHOTO | D. | Shape of the Vietnamese soldier's wound |
| Y - 5. | TED | E. | The listening ___ heard sounds foreign to the jungle. |
| L - 6. | EVIL | F. | It indirectly causes Kiowa's death. |
| C - 7. | KIOWA | G. | Norman asked the narrator to write Speaking Of ___. |
| U - 8. | GRUNT | H. | A war story is ____ if it embarrasses the listener. |
| T - 9. | GREEN | I. | Name of the Company |
| M - 10. | KATHLEEN | J. | The muddy field was full of this. |
| A - 11. | PANTYHOSE | K. | Aids O'Brien in getting revenge |
| N - 12. | IRONIC | L. | Narrator found it difficult to admit he was capable of this. |
| G - 13. | COURAGE | M. | O'Brien's daughter |
| R - 14. | JACKKNIFE | N. | Azar thought it was ___ to die in a field of excrement. |
| K - 15. | AZAR | O. | O'Brien's summer job in 1968 |
| V - 16. | HENRY | P. | Fainted during a dentist visit |
| H - 17. | TRUE | Q. | Norman didn't win the ___ Star. |
| I - 18. | ALPHA | R. | Object of Strunk and Jensen's fistfight |
| J - 19. | EXCREMENT | S. | Fourth-grade girlfriend of O'Brien |
| D - 20. | STAR | T. | The ___ Berets used the compound as their base. |
| B - 21. | TUMOR | U. | Any soldier |
| W - 22. | JUNGLE | V. | His girlfriend dumped him in October; monks liked him |
| O - 23. | DECLOTTER | W. | Mary Anne disappears into the ___. |
| S - 24. | LINDA | X. | Azar mocked this. |
| E - 25. | PATROL | Y. | Escapes the realities of the war by using drugs |

The Things They Carried Matching 3

___ 1. PISTOL           A. Fourth-grade girlfriend of O'Brien
___ 2. CARRIED          B. The ___ Berets used the compound as their base.
___ 3. LINDA            C. Confessed he made up parts of the story
___ 4. SISTER           D. Mary Anne was the ___ of the Song Tra Bong.
___ 5. RAT              E. To get killed
___ 6. VIETNAM          F. Country & name of the war
___ 7. SWEETHEART       G. Shape of the Vietnamese soldier's wound
___ 8. SPOOKED          H. Cause of Linda's demise
___ 9. DECLOTTER        I. Object that broke Jensen's nose
___10. TUMOR            J. The Things They ___
___11. LEMON            K. Jorgenson's job
___12. FOOT             L. Kiley shot himself there.
___13. STAR             M. Believes that stories can save lives
___14. PHOTO            N. O'Brien's summer job in 1968
___15. SANDERS          O. Rat wrote to Curt Lemon's
___16. BERDAHL          P. Hero of the narrator's life
___17. TRIP             Q. Known for exaggerating
___18. EXCREMENT        R. Dobbins threatens to put Azar in one.
___19. LODGE            S. It indirectly causes Kiowa's death.
___20. OBRIEN           T. The muddy field was full of this.
___21. GREEN            U. Narrator gave Kathleen a ___ to Vietnam as a present.
___22. WELL             V. Narrator drove to the Tip Top ___
___23. IRONIC           W. Fainted during a dentist visit
___24. JUNGLE           X. Mary Anne disappears into the ___.
___25. MEDIC            Y. Azar thought it was ___ to die in a field of excrement.

The Things They Carried Matching 3 Answer Key

| | | | |
|---|---|---|---|
| I - | 1. PISTOL | A. | Fourth-grade girlfriend of O'Brien |
| J - | 2. CARRIED | B. | The ___ Berets used the compound as their base. |
| A - | 3. LINDA | C. | Confessed he made up parts of the story |
| O - | 4. SISTER | D. | Mary Anne was the ___ of the Song Tra Bong. |
| Q - | 5. RAT | E. | To get killed |
| F - | 6. VIETNAM | F. | Country & name of the war |
| D - | 7. SWEETHEART | G. | Shape of the Vietnamese soldier's wound |
| E - | 8. SPOOKED | H. | Cause of Linda's demise |
| N - | 9. DECLOTTER | I. | Object that broke Jensen's nose |
| H - | 10. TUMOR | J. | The Things They ___ |
| W - | 11. LEMON | K. | Jorgenson's job |
| L - | 12. FOOT | L. | Kiley shot himself there. |
| G - | 13. STAR | M. | Believes that stories can save lives |
| S - | 14. PHOTO | N. | O'Brien's summer job in 1968 |
| C - | 15. SANDERS | O. | Rat wrote to Curt Lemon's |
| P - | 16. BERDAHL | P. | Hero of the narrator's life |
| U - | 17. TRIP | Q. | Known for exaggerating |
| T - | 18. EXCREMENT | R. | Dobbins threatens to put Azar in one. |
| V - | 19. LODGE | S. | It indirectly causes Kiowa's death. |
| M - | 20. OBRIEN | T. | The muddy field was full of this. |
| B - | 21. GREEN | U. | Narrator gave Kathleen a ___ to Vietnam as a present. |
| R - | 22. WELL | V. | Narrator drove to the Tip Top ___ |
| Y - | 23. IRONIC | W. | Fainted during a dentist visit |
| X - | 24. JUNGLE | X. | Mary Anne disappears into the ___. |
| K - | 25. MEDIC | Y. | Azar thought it was ___ to die in a field of excrement. |

The Things They Carried Matching 4

___ 1. COURAGE          A. Aids O'Brien in getting revenge
___ 2. MARTHA           B. To get killed
___ 3. JACKKNIFE        C. Shape of the Vietnamese soldier's wound
___ 4. EXCREMENT        D. Hero of the narrator's life
___ 5. STAR             E. Object of Strunk and Jensen's fistfight
___ 6. AZAR             F. Rat wrote to Curt Lemon's
___ 7. TRIP             G. A war story is ____ if it embarrasses the listener.
___ 8. SWEETHEART       H. Fourth-grade girlfriend of O'Brien
___ 9. BERDAHL          I. Narrator gave Kathleen a ___ to Vietnam as a present.
___ 10. KATHLEEN        J. Azar thought it was ___ to die in a field of excrement.
___ 11. SILVER          K. The ___ Berets used the compound as their base.
___ 12. NOSE            L. Kiowa advised soldiers not to damage or profane these.
___ 13. VIETNAM         M. Kiley shot himself there.
___ 14. SPOOKED         N. Lt. Cross burned her picture
___ 15. IRONIC          O. Mary Anne was the ___ of the Song Tra Bong.
___ 16. LINDA           P. Country & name of the war
___ 17. TRUE            Q. Jensen broke his own
___ 18. GREEN           R. The muddy field was full of this.
___ 19. FOOT            S. Norman drove around it.
___ 20. LAKE            T. Note with money in envelope said Emergency ___.
___ 21. CORPSE          U. O'Brien's daughter
___ 22. CHURCHES        V. Narrator refused to shake hands with one
___ 23. SISTER          W. Norman asked the narrator to write Speaking Of ___.
___ 24. FUND            X. Mark compromised with Mary Anne and they became ___.
___ 25. ENGAGED         Y. Norman didn't win the ___ Star.

The Things They Carried Matching 4 Answer Key

| | | | |
|---|---|---|---|
| W - 1. | COURAGE | A. | Aids O'Brien in getting revenge |
| N - 2. | MARTHA | B. | To get killed |
| E - 3. | JACKKNIFE | C. | Shape of the Vietnamese soldier's wound |
| R - 4. | EXCREMENT | D. | Hero of the narrator's life |
| C - 5. | STAR | E. | Object of Strunk and Jensen's fistfight |
| A - 6. | AZAR | F. | Rat wrote to Curt Lemon's |
| I - 7. | TRIP | G. | A war story is ____ if it embarrasses the listener. |
| O - 8. | SWEETHEART | H. | Fourth-grade girlfriend of O'Brien |
| D - 9. | BERDAHL | I. | Narrator gave Kathleen a ___ to Vietnam as a present. |
| U -10. | KATHLEEN | J. | Azar thought it was ___ to die in a field of excrement. |
| Y -11. | SILVER | K. | The ___ Berets used the compound as their base. |
| Q -12. | NOSE | L. | Kiowa advised soldiers not to damage or profane these. |
| P -13. | VIETNAM | M. | Kiley shot himself there. |
| B -14. | SPOOKED | N. | Lt. Cross burned her picture |
| J -15. | IRONIC | O. | Mary Anne was the ___ of the Song Tra Bong. |
| H -16. | LINDA | P. | Country & name of the war |
| G -17. | TRUE | Q. | Jensen broke his own |
| K -18. | GREEN | R. | The muddy field was full of this. |
| M -19. | FOOT | S. | Norman drove around it. |
| S -20. | LAKE | T. | Note with money in envelope said Emergency ___. |
| V -21. | CORPSE | U. | O'Brien's daughter |
| L -22. | CHURCHES | V. | Narrator refused to shake hands with one |
| F -23. | SISTER | W. | Norman asked the narrator to write Speaking Of ___. |
| T -24. | FUND | X. | Mark compromised with Mary Anne and they became ___. |
| X -25. | ENGAGED | Y. | Norman didn't win the ___ Star. |

The Things They Carried Magic Squares 1

Match the definition with the vocabulary word. Put your answers in the magic squares below. When your answers are correct, all columns and rows will add to the same number.

A. LODGE
B. OBRIEN
C. VIETNAM
D. ENGAGED
E. SWEETHEART
F. FUND
G. SANDERS
H. PISTOL
I. MARTHA
J. PHOTO
K. SISTER
L. PANTYHOSE
M. WELL
N. LAKE
O. NOSE
P. DECLOTTER

1. Norman drove around it.
2. Confessed he made up parts of the story
3. Good-luck item for Dobbins
4. Narrator drove to the Tip Top ___
5. Rat wrote to Curt Lemon's
6. Believes that stories can save lives
7. Dobbins threatens to put Azar in one.
8. Object that broke Jensen's nose
9. Mary Anne was the ___ of the Song Tra Bong.
10. O'Brien's summer job in 1968
11. Country & name of the war
12. It indirectly causes Kiowa's death.
13. Mark compromised with Mary Anne and they became ___.
14. Lt. Cross burned her picture
15. Note with money in envelope said Emergency ___.
16. Jensen broke his own

| A= | B= | C= | D= |
| --- | --- | --- | --- |
| E= | F= | G= | H= |
| I= | J= | K= | L= |
| M= | N= | O= | P= |

The Things They Carried Magic Squares 1 Answer Key

Match the definition with the vocabulary word. Put your answers in the magic squares below. When your answers are correct, all columns and rows will add to the same number.

A. LODGE
B. OBRIEN
C. VIETNAM
D. ENGAGED
E. SWEETHEART
F. FUND
G. SANDERS
H. PISTOL
I. MARTHA
J. PHOTO
K. SISTER
L. PANTYHOSE
M. WELL
N. LAKE
O. NOSE
P. DECLOTTER

1. Norman drove around it.
2. Confessed he made up parts of the story
3. Good-luck item for Dobbins
4. Narrator drove to the Tip Top ___
5. Rat wrote to Curt Lemon's
6. Believes that stories can save lives
7. Dobbins threatens to put Azar in one.
8. Object that broke Jensen's nose
9. Mary Anne was the ___ of the Song Tra Bong.
10. O'Brien's summer job in 1968
11. Country & name of the war
12. It indirectly causes Kiowa's death.
13. Mark compromised with Mary Anne and they became ___.
14. Lt. Cross burned her picture
15. Note with money in envelope said Emergency ___.
16. Jensen broke his own

| A=4 | B=6 | C=11 | D=13 |
| --- | --- | --- | --- |
| E=9 | F=15 | G=2 | H=8 |
| I=14 | J=12 | K=5 | L=3 |
| M=7 | N=1 | O=16 | P=10 |

The Things They Carried Magic Squares 2

Match the definition with the vocabulary word. Put your answers in the magic squares below. When your answers are correct, all columns and rows will add to the same number.

A. BERDAHL   E. CARRIED   I. AZAR      M. FUND
B. FOSSE     F. TRUE      J. COURAGE   N. LAKE
C. JUNGLE    G. LINDA     K. PISTOL    O. IRONIC
D. CANADA    H. SPOOKED   L. MEDIC     P. ALPHA

1. To get killed
2. Hero of the narrator's life
3. Brought his girlfriend to Vietnam for a visit
4. Fourth-grade girlfriend of O'Brien
5. Norman asked the narrator to write Speaking Of ___.
6. Azar thought it was ___ to die in a field of excrement.
7. Name of the Company
8. Aids O'Brien in getting revenge
9. Object that broke Jensen's nose
10. Norman drove around it.
11. Note with money in envelope said Emergency ___.
12. Jorgenson's job
13. The Things They ___
14. Place many draft-dodgers fled to
15. Mary Anne disappears into the ___.
16. A war story is ___ if it embarrasses the listener.

| A= | B= | C= | D= |
| E= | F= | G= | H= |
| I= | J= | K= | L= |
| M= | N= | O= | P= |

The Things They Carried Magic Squares 2 Answer Key

Match the definition with the vocabulary word. Put your answers in the magic squares below. When your answers are correct, all columns and rows will add to the same number.

A. BERDAHL     E. CARRIED     I. AZAR        M. FUND
B. FOSSE       F. TRUE        J. COURAGE     N. LAKE
C. JUNGLE      G. LINDA       K. PISTOL      O. IRONIC
D. CANADA      H. SPOOKED     L. MEDIC       P. ALPHA

1. To get killed
2. Hero of the narrator's life
3. Brought his girlfriend to Vietnam for a visit
4. Fourth-grade girlfriend of O'Brien
5. Norman asked the narrator to write Speaking Of ___.
6. Azar thought it was ___ to die in a field of excrement.
7. Name of the Company
8. Aids O'Brien in getting revenge
9. Object that broke Jensen's nose
10. Norman drove around it.
11. Note with money in envelope said Emergency ___.
12. Jorgenson's job
13. The Things They ___
14. Place many draft-dodgers fled to
15. Mary Anne disappears into the ___.
16. A war story is ___ if it embarrasses the listener.

| A=2 | B=3 | C=15 | D=14 |
| --- | --- | --- | --- |
| E=13 | F=16 | G=4 | H=1 |
| I=8 | J=5 | K=9 | L=12 |
| M=11 | N=10 | O=6 | P=7 |

The Things They Carried Magic Squares 3

Match the definition with the vocabulary word. Put your answers in the magic squares below. When your answers are correct, all columns and rows will add to the same number.

A. ALPHA
B. BOWKER
C. HUMP
D. PATROL
E. STORIES
F. LAKE
G. TRUE
H. SWEETHEART
I. CANADA
J. CHURCHES
K. DECLOTTER
L. LEMON
M. TUMOR
N. DANCING
O. IRONIC
P. BUFFALO

1. Norman drove around it.
2. Place many draft-dodgers fled to
3. Azar thought it was ___ to die in a field of excrement.
4. The listening ___ heard sounds foreign to the jungle.
5. Cause of Linda's demise
6. Commits suicide
7. Mary Anne was the ___ of the Song Tra Bong.
8. O'Brien's summer job in 1968
9. To carry
10. Water ___ was killed because of Rat's grief
11. Kiowa advised soldiers not to damage or profane these.
12. Tim tries to save Timmy's life using these.
13. Fainted during a dentist visit
14. A war story is ___ if it embarrasses the listener.
15. Name of the Company
16. Azar mocked this.

| A= | B= | C= | D= |
| E= | F= | G= | H= |
| I= | J= | K= | L= |
| M= | N= | O= | P= |

The Things They Carried Magic Squares 3 Answer Key

Match the definition with the vocabulary word. Put your answers in the magic squares below. When your answers are correct, all columns and rows will add to the same number.

A. ALPHA
B. BOWKER
C. HUMP
D. PATROL
E. STORIES
F. LAKE
G. TRUE
H. SWEETHEART
I. CANADA
J. CHURCHES
K. DECLOTTER
L. LEMON
M. TUMOR
N. DANCING
O. IRONIC
P. BUFFALO

1. Norman drove around it.
2. Place many draft-dodgers fled to
3. Azar thought it was ___ to die in a field of excrement.
4. The listening ___ heard sounds foreign to the jungle.
5. Cause of Linda's demise
6. Commits suicide
7. Mary Anne was the ___ of the Song Tra Bong.
8. O'Brien's summer job in 1968
9. To carry
10. Water ___ was killed because of Rat's grief
11. Kiowa advised soldiers not to damage or profane these.
12. Tim tries to save Timmy's life using these.
13. Fainted during a dentist visit
14. A war story is ___ if it embarrasses the listener.
15. Name of the Company
16. Azar mocked this.

| A=15 | B=6  | C=9  | D=4  |
| ---- | ---- | ---- | ---- |
| E=12 | F=1  | G=14 | H=7  |
| I=2  | J=11 | K=8  | L=13 |
| M=5  | N=16 | O=3  | P=10 |

The Things They Carried Magic Squares 4

Match the definition with the vocabulary word. Put your answers in the magic squares below. When your answers are correct, all columns and rows will add to the same number.

A. EXCREMENT	E. SANK	I. ALPHA	M. STORIES
B. VIETNAM	F. MEDIC	J. STAR	N. PATROL
C. GRUNT	G. TRUE	K. PHOTO	O. LODGE
D. JACKKNIFE	H. LINDA	L. TUMOR	P. MOCCASINS

1. Fourth-grade girlfriend of O'Brien
2. Tim tries to save Timmy's life using these.
3. Country & name of the war
4. It indirectly causes Kiowa's death.
5. Shape of the Vietnamese soldier's wound
6. Any soldier
7. Kiowa's were in the rucksack.
8. Kiowa ___ into the mud.
9. Narrator drove to the Tip Top ___
10. Jorgenson's job
11. Name of the Company
12. Object of Strunk and Jensen's fistfight
13. The muddy field was full of this.
14. Cause of Linda's demise
15. A war story is ____ if it embarrasses the listener.
16. The listening ___ heard sounds foreign to the jungle.

| A= | B= | C= | D= |
| E= | F= | G= | H= |
| I= | J= | K= | L= |
| M= | N= | O= | P= |

The Things They Carried Magic Squares 4 Answer Key

Match the definition with the vocabulary word. Put your answers in the magic squares below. When your answers are correct, all columns and rows will add to the same number.

A. EXCREMENT  E. SANK    I. ALPHA   M. STORIES
B. VIETNAM    F. MEDIC   J. STAR    N. PATROL
C. GRUNT      G. TRUE    K. PHOTO   O. LODGE
D. JACKKNIFE  H. LINDA   L. TUMOR   P. MOCCASINS

1. Fourth-grade girlfriend of O'Brien
2. Tim tries to save Timmy's life using these.
3. Country & name of the war
4. It indirectly causes Kiowa's death.
5. Shape of the Vietnamese soldier's wound
6. Any soldier
7. Kiowa's were in the rucksack.
8. Kiowa ___ into the mud.
9. Narrator drove to the Tip Top ___
10. Jorgenson's job
11. Name of the Company
12. Object of Strunk and Jensen's fistfight
13. The muddy field was full of this.
14. Cause of Linda's demise
15. A war story is ____ if it embarrasses the listener.
16. The listening ___ heard sounds foreign to the jungle.

| A=13 | B=3  | C=6  | D=12 |
| E=8  | F=10 | G=15 | H=1  |
| I=11 | J=5  | K=4  | L=14 |
| M=2  | N=16 | O=9  | P=7  |

29
Copyrighted

The Things They Carried Word Search 1

```
P A N T Y H O S E J A C K K N I F E
H A L M X X K T R I C G P I B G V T
U P T E V F B A Q D R S P O O K E D
M J N R M M A R T H A O V W L A K E
P O K D O O R T Z H J N N A X X D R
J S C D B L N J J N L P C I Z R J R
C I J C N O D S S G L E B I C V U X
E L K W A N B Y Z N C I E O N J N R
F V H E R S S R W O F A N N W G G F
U E I L X C I E I S H F R D R K L X
N R A L P H A N P E C O U R A G E N
D E L N T U G G S I N O L A I R L R
T M W G S R R A H T S T R T B E O S
E M E D I C U G Z E O T F P M E D V
D X G M S H N E C A N R O O S N G M
R H L K T E T D Y P R R I L S E E G
T R I P E S C A N A D A Y E H S K Z
T U M O R P H O T O S A N K S V E X
```

A war story is ____ if it embarrasses the listener. (4)
Aids O'Brien in getting revenge (4)
Any soldier (5)
Azar mocked this. (7)
Azar thought it was ___ to die in a field of excrement. (6)
Believes that stories can save lives (6)
Brought his girlfriend to Vietnam for a visit (5)
Cause of Linda's demise (5)
Commits suicide (6)
Dobbins threatens to put Azar in one. (4)
Escapes the realities of the war by using drugs (3)
Fainted during a dentist visit (5)
Fourth-grade girlfriend of O'Brien (5)
Good-luck item for Dobbins (9)
His girlfriend dumped him in October; monks liked him (5)
It indirectly causes Kiowa's death. (5)
Jensen broke his own (4)
Jorgenson's job (5)
Kiley shot himself there. (4)
Kiowa ___ into the mud. (4)
Kiowa advised soldiers not to damage or profane these. (8)
Kiowa received an illustrated ___ Testament. (3)
Kiowa's were in the rucksack. (9)
Known for exaggerating (3)
Lt. Cross burned her picture (6)
Mark compromised with Mary Anne and they became ___. (7)
Mary Anne disappears into the ___. (6)
Name of the Company (5)
Narrator drove to the Tip Top ___ (5)
Narrator found it difficult to admit he was capable of this. (4)
Narrator gave Kathleen a ___ to Vietnam as a present. (4)
Narrator refused to shake hands with one (6)
Native American soldier (5)
Norman asked the narrator to write Speaking Of ___. (7)
Norman didn't win the ___ Star. (6)
Norman drove around it. (4)
Note with money in envelope said Emergency ___. (4)
O'Brien's daughter (8)
Object of Strunk and Jensen's fistfight (9)
Object that broke Jensen's nose (6)
Place many draft-dodgers fled to (6)
Rat wrote to Curt Lemon's (6)
Shape of the Vietnamese soldier's wound (4)
The Things They ___ (7)
The ___ Berets used the compound as their base. (5)
The listening ___ heard sounds foreign to the jungle. (6)
Tim tries to save Timmy's life using these. (7)
To carry (4)
To get killed (7)

The Things They Carried Word Search 1 Answer Key

```
P  A  N  T  Y  H  O  S  E  J  A  C  K  K  N  I  F  E
H  A  L        K  T        I           I
U     L  T  E        A     D  R  S  P  O     K  E  D
M           R  M  M  A  R  T  H  A  O     W  L  A  K  E
P  O           O  O           H     N  N  A
   S  C           L  N              L     C           J
      I     C        O              L  E  B  I  C     U
E     L     W  A     B        N     C  I  E  O  N     N
F  V        E        S  R     O        A  N  N  W  G
U  E  I     L        C  I  E  I        F  R  D     K  L
N  R  A  L     P  H  A  N  P  E  C  O  U  R  A  G  E
D  E           T  U  G  G  S  I  N  O     A  I  R  L     R
T     W        S  R  R  A  H  T  S  T  R  T     E  O
E  M  E  D  I  C  U  G  Z  E  O  T  F  P     E  D
D           S  H  N  E     A  N  R  O  O  S  N  G
            T  E  T  D        R  R  I  L  S  E  E
T  R  I  P  E  S  C  A  N  A  D  A  Y  E     S
T  U  M  O  R  P  H  O  T  O  S  A  N  K  S        E
```

A war story is ____ if it embarrasses the listener. (4)
Aids O'Brien in getting revenge (4)
Any soldier (5)
Azar mocked this. (7)
Azar thought it was ___ to die in a field of excrement. (6)
Believes that stories can save lives (6)
Brought his girlfriend to Vietnam for a visit (5)
Cause of Linda's demise (5)
Commits suicide (6)
Dobbins threatens to put Azar in one. (4)
Escapes the realities of the war by using drugs (3)
Fainted during a dentist visit (5)
Fourth-grade girlfriend of O'Brien (5)
Good-luck item for Dobbins (9)
His girlfriend dumped him in October; monks liked him (5)
It indirectly causes Kiowa's death. (5)
Jensen broke his own (4)
Jorgenson's job (5)
Kiley shot himself there. (4)
Kiowa ___ into the mud. (4)
Kiowa advised soldiers not to damage or profane these. (8)
Kiowa received an illustrated ___ Testament. (3)
Kiowa's were in the rucksack. (9)
Known for exaggerating (3)
Lt. Cross burned her picture (6)
Mark compromised with Mary Anne and they became ___. (7)
Mary Anne disappears into the ___. (6)
Name of the Company (5)
Narrator drove to the Tip Top ___ (5)
Narrator found it difficult to admit he was capable of this. (4)
Narrator gave Kathleen a ___ to Vietnam as a present. (4)
Narrator refused to shake hands with one (6)
Native American soldier (5)
Norman asked the narrator to write Speaking Of ___. (7)
Norman didn't win the ___ Star. (6)
Norman drove around it. (4)
Note with money in envelope said Emergency ___. (4)
O'Brien's daughter (8)
Object of Strunk and Jensen's fistfight (9)
Object that broke Jensen's nose (6)
Place many draft-dodgers fled to (6)
Rat wrote to Curt Lemon's (6)
Shape of the Vietnamese soldier's wound (4)
The Things They ___ (7)
The ___ Berets used the compound as their base. (5)
The listening ___ heard sounds foreign to the jungle. (6)
Tim tries to save Timmy's life using these. (7)
To carry (4)
To get killed (7)

# The Things They Carried Word Search 2

```
E V I L L C J V D J J V M F L B G M
A L P H A A K A E V J L O S I U Z L
G H W X K N I P C C N A C D N F Z D
T R V F E A O S L K N V C N D F S Y
S P U U F D W I O T K E A F A A T P
F H S N K A A S T W P N S G O L A V
Q O G D T E D T T M E D I C R O R D
C T S R R V Q E E O F E N F N E T D
W O H S U G S R R M R R S L E C E P
K J M W E H A L J K C I L Z C O T N
A Z A R P A N T Y H O S E N B R R Z
T J T A P I K E F U U P M S O P I W
H H U T I A S K W M R O O Z W S P M
L L M N W R T T L P A O N P K E E K
E H O X G E O R O Y G K J H E N R Y
E H R D T L L N O L E E O B R I E N
N N D W G P E L I L F D A N C I N G
X S I L V E R T W C H U R C H E S Z
```

A war story is ____ if it embarrasses the listener. (4)
Aids O'Brien in getting revenge (4)
Any soldier (5)
Azar mocked this. (7)
Azar thought it was ___ to die in a field of excrement. (6)
Believes that stories can save lives (6)
Brought his girlfriend to Vietnam for a visit (5)
Cause of Linda's demise (5)
Commits suicide (6)
Dobbins threatens to put Azar in one. (4)
Escapes the realities of the war by using drugs (3)
Fainted during a dentist visit (5)
Fourth-grade girlfriend of O'Brien (5)
Good-luck item for Dobbins (9)
His girlfriend dumped him in October; monks liked him (5)
It indirectly causes Kiowa's death. (5)
Jensen broke his own (4)
Jimmy Cross never forgave himself for this soldier's death. (8)
Jorgenson's job (5)
Kiley shot himself there. (4)
Kiowa ___ into the mud. (4)
Kiowa advised soldiers not to damage or profane these. (8)
Kiowa received an illustrated ___ Testament. (3)
Kiowa's were in the rucksack. (9)
Known for exaggerating (3)
Mary Anne disappears into the ___. (6)
Name of the Company (5)
Narrator drove to the Tip Top ___ (5)
Narrator found it difficult to admit he was capable of this. (4)
Narrator gave Kathleen a ___ to Vietnam as a present. (4)
Narrator refused to shake hands with one (6)
Native American soldier (5)
Norman asked the narrator to write Speaking Of ___. (7)
Norman didn't win the ___ Star. (6)
Norman drove around it. (4)
Note with money in envelope said Emergency ___. (4)
O'Brien's daughter (8)
O'Brien's summer job in 1968 (9)
Object of Strunk and Jensen's fistfight (9)
Object that broke Jensen's nose (6)
Place many draft-dodgers fled to (6)
Rat wrote to Curt Lemon's (6)
Shape of the Vietnamese soldier's wound (4)
The ___ Berets used the compound as their base. (5)
The listening ___ heard sounds foreign to the jungle. (6)
Tim tries to save Timmy's life using these. (7)
To carry (4)
To get killed (7)
Water ___ was killed because of Rat's grief (7)

The Things They Carried Word Search 2 Answer Key

```
E  V  I  L  L  C  J     D        M     L  B
A  L  P  H  A  A  K  A  E        O     I  U
G           K  N  I     C        A  C     N  F
   R     F  E  A  O  S  L  K     V  C     D  F  S
   P  U  U     D  W  I  O     K  E  A  F  A  A  T
F  H     N     A  A  S  T        N  S  G  O  L  A
   O     D  T  E  D  T  T  M  E  D  I  C  R  O  R
   T  S     R        E  E  O     E  N  F     E  T
   O     S  U     S  R  R        R  S     E  C  E
K           E     A           C  I  L        O  T  N
A  Z  A  R  P  A  N  T  Y  H  O  S  E  N  B  R  R
T  J  T  A  P  I  K  E     U  U  P  M  S  O  P  I
H     U  T  I  A  S     W  M  R  O     W  S  P
L  L  M  N  W  R  T  T     P  A  O  N     K  E  E
E     O     G  E  O  R  O     G  K     H  E  N  R  Y
E     R  D     L  L  N  O  L  E  E  O  B  R  I  E  N
N              G     E  L  L     D  A  N  C  I  N  G
      S  I  L  V  E  R        C  H  U  R  C  H  E  S
```

A war story is ____ if it embarrasses the listener. (4)
Aids O'Brien in getting revenge (4)
Any soldier (5)
Azar mocked this. (7)
Azar thought it was ____ to die in a field of excrement. (6)
Believes that stories can save lives (6)
Brought his girlfriend to Vietnam for a visit (5)
Cause of Linda's demise (5)
Commits suicide (6)
Dobbins threatens to put Azar in one. (4)
Escapes the realities of the war by using drugs (3)
Fainted during a dentist visit (5)
Fourth-grade girlfriend of O'Brien (5)
Good-luck item for Dobbins (9)
His girlfriend dumped him in October; monks liked him (5)
It indirectly causes Kiowa's death. (5)
Jensen broke his own (4)
Jimmy Cross never forgave himself for this soldier's death. (8)
Jorgenson's job (5)
Kiley shot himself there. (4)
Kiowa ____ into the mud. (4)
Kiowa advised soldiers not to damage or profane these. (8)
Kiowa received an illustrated ____ Testament. (3)
Kiowa's were in the rucksack. (9)
Known for exaggerating (3)
Mary Anne disappears into the ____. (6)
Name of the Company (5)
Narrator drove to the Tip Top ____ (5)
Narrator found it difficult to admit he was capable of this. (4)
Narrator gave Kathleen a ____ to Vietnam as a present. (4)
Narrator refused to shake hands with one (6)
Native American soldier (5)
Norman asked the narrator to write Speaking Of ____. (7)
Norman didn't win the ____ Star. (6)
Norman drove around it. (4)
Note with money in envelope said Emergency ____. (4)
O'Brien's daughter (8)
O'Brien's summer job in 1968 (9)
Object of Strunk and Jensen's fistfight (9)
Object that broke Jensen's nose (6)
Place many draft-dodgers fled to (6)
Rat wrote to Curt Lemon's (6)
Shape of the Vietnamese soldier's wound (4)
The ____ Berets used the compound as their base. (5)
The listening ____ heard sounds foreign to the jungle. (6)
Tim tries to save Timmy's life using these. (7)
To carry (4)
To get killed (7)
Water ____ was killed because of Rat's grief (7)

The Things They Carried Word Search 3

```
L A Z A R F O O T T B R S K I L E M O N
O N L D X D B N Q Z O P A T K R A M S W
D E A N T A G K W S W A N T O G O K K Y
G W V J U N G L E X K N D P V R H N E B
E S E C M C C Q S Q E T E A I E I B I K
J T N A O I O S K P R Y R T E E J E N C
K A D N R N R T I T O H S R T N A K S D
Z R E A T G P P I S T O L O N O C A C R
H W R D R F S G M B T S K L A B K T A J
Z E Z A I Y E H W A U E Q E M R K H R M
N L V Z P X P U Y Z R F R X D I N L R Y
N L E X C R E M E N T T F W E E I E I J
F F P S X V M P G M T C H A C N F E E C
V C X P Z K H S Y Z F T W A L W E N D N
N X H M M G W V G B K M B H O O Q G S V
N C O U R A G E T T C W H R T C S P W W
H M Q F R B P X P L B W Q R T M P B E R
J B L C F C E F W I C K Y E E L H F E B
S X W H T G H R W N F R B N R X O O T J
M J S F W S K E D D L P S G H C T S H K
M O C C A S I N S A L P H A F N O S E N
N W Y W J N O L B S H Z D G N P B E A S
C X Q C N H W G V L L L T E H K N F R H
G R U N T R A B M E D I C D E V I L T B
T E D F U N D P Y S R T R U E H E N R Y
```

| ALPHA | ENGAGED | JUNGLE | NOSE | STAR |
| AZAR | EVIL | KATHLEEN | OBRIEN | STORIES |
| BERDAHL | EXCREMENT | KIOWA | PANTYHOSE | SWEETHEART |
| BOWKER | FOOT | LAKE | PATROL | TED |
| BUFFALO | FOSSE | LAVENDER | PHOTO | TRIP |
| CANADA | FUND | LEMON | PISTOL | TRUE |
| CARRIED | GREEN | LINDA | RAT | TUMOR |
| CHURCHES | GRUNT | LODGE | SANDERS | VIETNAM |
| CORPSE | HENRY | MARTHA | SANK | WELL |
| COURAGE | HUMP | MEDIC | SILVER | |
| DANCING | IRONIC | MOCCASINS | SISTER | |
| DECLOTTER | JACKKNIFE | NEW | SPOOKED | |

The Things They Carried Word Search 3 Answer Key

| ALPHA | ENGAGED | JUNGLE | NOSE | STAR |
| AZAR | EVIL | KATHLEEN | OBRIEN | STORIES |
| BERDAHL | EXCREMENT | KIOWA | PANTYHOSE | SWEETHEART |
| BOWKER | FOOT | LAKE | PATROL | TED |
| BUFFALO | FOSSE | LAVENDER | PHOTO | TRIP |
| CANADA | FUND | LEMON | PISTOL | TRUE |
| CARRIED | GREEN | LINDA | RAT | TUMOR |
| CHURCHES | GRUNT | LODGE | SANDERS | VIETNAM |
| CORPSE | HENRY | MARTHA | SANK | WELL |
| COURAGE | HUMP | MEDIC | SILVER | |
| DANCING | IRONIC | MOCCASINS | SISTER | |
| DECLOTTER | JACKKNIFE | NEW | SPOOKED | |

# The Things They Carried Word Search 4

```
S S Q D C K P S W E E T H E A R T W Q F
J K S E Q R A C T M C S R G R W W S H M
D A P C C X N D H V H O F D F F H I M K
Y T Y L M M T Y P G G N R R H B H S E B
M H B O E Z Y L Y L R T S P A H U T D Y
F L O T V M H R L R L U A M S L M E I M
N E W T Z M O C C A S I N S T E P R C F
F E K E W M S N A T V T K T E V T H G Y
N N E R L W E J R X R E O A D I R J A K
K M R W C L M C R M L P N R Q L I A H C
F M H P H O T O I A Z A R D I F P C K X
P U G V U C J U E T G T K L E E X K I L
D X N B R D U R D R Y R W E P R S K O D
B G H D C L N A H U B O E T Q F W N W S
S U J B H Y G G W E C L D E L O B I A Q
I A F H E M L E X J N A P A N O R F D Z
L D N F S R E G L P I R N I N T R E J X
V L H D A E D K X W R P Y A S C D P L R
E N O S E L N A T F O S S E D T I D Y X
R R V P H R O G H T N B V K L A O N H T
L Z F O G Y S T A L I C R L L X L L G M
I S Y O W M J U K G C B K I L O D G E V
N X W K N G W M B G E P V I E T N A M G
D T D E H N D O N C G D V P N N Y G F R
A B B D E X C R E M E N T M A R T H A B
```

| ALPHA | ENGAGED | JUNGLE | NOSE | STAR |
| AZAR | EVIL | KATHLEEN | OBRIEN | STORIES |
| BERDAHL | EXCREMENT | KIOWA | PANTYHOSE | SWEETHEART |
| BOWKER | FOOT | LAKE | PATROL | TED |
| BUFFALO | FOSSE | LAVENDER | PHOTO | TRIP |
| CANADA | FUND | LEMON | PISTOL | TRUE |
| CARRIED | GREEN | LINDA | RAT | TUMOR |
| CHURCHES | GRUNT | LODGE | SANDERS | VIETNAM |
| CORPSE | HENRY | MARTHA | SANK | WELL |
| COURAGE | HUMP | MEDIC | SILVER | |
| DANCING | IRONIC | MOCCASINS | SISTER | |
| DECLOTTER | JACKKNIFE | NEW | SPOOKED | |

The Things They Carried Word Search 4 Answer Key

| ALPHA | ENGAGED | JUNGLE | NOSE | STAR |
| AZAR | EVIL | KATHLEEN | OBRIEN | STORIES |
| BERDAHL | EXCREMENT | KIOWA | PANTYHOSE | SWEETHEART |
| BOWKER | FOOT | LAKE | PATROL | TED |
| BUFFALO | FOSSE | LAVENDER | PHOTO | TRIP |
| CANADA | FUND | LEMON | PISTOL | TRUE |
| CARRIED | GREEN | LINDA | RAT | TUMOR |
| CHURCHES | GRUNT | LODGE | SANDERS | VIETNAM |
| CORPSE | HENRY | MARTHA | SANK | WELL |
| COURAGE | HUMP | MEDIC | SILVER | |
| DANCING | IRONIC | MOCCASINS | SISTER | |
| DECLOTTER | JACKKNIFE | NEW | SPOOKED | |

The Things They Carried Crossword 1

Across
1. Azar mocked this.
5. A war story is ____ if it embarrasses the listener.
6. Known for exaggerating
8. Note with money in envelope said Emergency ____.
9. Kiley shot himself there.
10. Aids O'Brien in getting revenge
12. Shape of the Vietnamese soldier's wound
13. To get killed
16. Narrator found it difficult to admit he was capable of this.
19. Believes that stories can save lives
20. Lt. Cross burned her picture
24. Hero of the narrator's life
25. Fourth-grade girlfriend of O'Brien
26. Dobbins threatens to put Azar in one.
27. Jorgenson's job

Down
1. O'Brien's summer job in 1968
2. Jensen broke his own
3. Any soldier
4. Water ____ was killed because of Rat's grief
5. Escapes the realities of the war by using drugs
7. Confessed he made up parts of the story
8. Brought his girlfriend to Vietnam for a visit
11. The ____ Berets used the compound as their base.
14. The listening ____ heard sounds foreign to the jungle.
15. Commits suicide
17. Country & name of the war
18. Fainted during a dentist visit
21. His girlfriend dumped him in October; monks liked him
22. Norman drove around it.
23. Kiowa ____ into the mud.

# The Things They Carried Crossword 1 Answer Key

**Across**
1. Azar mocked this.
5. A war story is ____ if it embarrasses the listener.
6. Known for exaggerating
8. Note with money in envelope said Emergency ____.
9. Kiley shot himself there.
10. Aids O'Brien in getting revenge
12. Shape of the Vietnamese soldier's wound
13. To get killed
16. Narrator found it difficult to admit he was capable of this.
19. Believes that stories can save lives
20. Lt. Cross burned her picture
24. Hero of the narrator's life
25. Fourth-grade girlfriend of O'Brien
26. Dobbins threatens to put Azar in one.
27. Jorgenson's job

**Down**
1. O'Brien's summer job in 1968
2. Jensen broke his own
3. Any soldier
4. Water ____ was killed because of Rat's grief
5. Escapes the realities of the war by using drugs
7. Confessed he made up parts of the story
8. Brought his girlfriend to Vietnam for a visit
11. The ____ Berets used the compound as their base.
14. The listening ____ heard sounds foreign to the jungle.
15. Commits suicide
17. Country & name of the war
18. Fainted during a dentist visit
21. His girlfriend dumped him in October; monks liked him
22. Norman drove around it.
23. Kiowa ____ into the mud.

# The Things They Carried Crossword 2

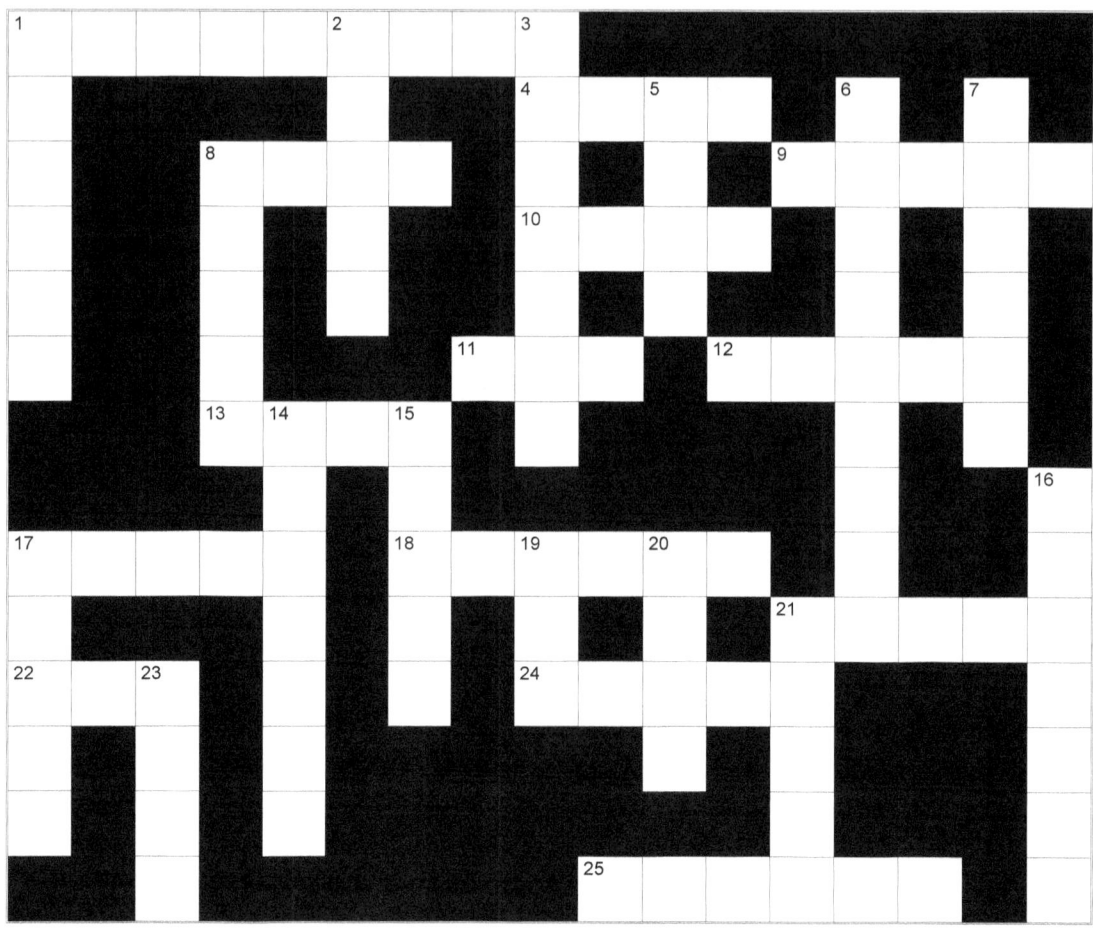

**Across**
1. Good-luck item for Dobbins
4. Jensen broke his own
8. Note with money in envelope said Emergency ___.
9. Jorgenson's job
10. Aids O'Brien in getting revenge
11. Escapes the realities of the war by using drugs
12. It indirectly causes Kiowa's death.
13. Narrator found it difficult to admit he was capable of this.
17. Narrator drove to the Tip Top ___
18. Lt. Cross burned her picture
21. The ___ Berets used the compound as their base.
22. Kiowa received an illustrated ___ Testament.
24. Cause of Linda's demise
25. Rat wrote to Curt Lemon's ___.

**Down**
1. The listening ___ heard sounds foreign to the jungle.
2. His girlfriend dumped him in October; monks liked him
3. Mark compromised with Mary Anne and they became ___.
5. Shape of the Vietnamese soldier's wound
6. O'Brien's summer job in 1968
7. Object that broke Jensen's nose
8. Brought his girlfriend to Vietnam for a visit
14. Country & name of the war
15. Fainted during a dentist visit
16. Confessed he made up parts of the story
17. Fourth-grade girlfriend of O'Brien
19. Known for exaggerating
20. To carry
21. Any soldier
23. Dobbins threatens to put Azar in one.

The Things They Carried Crossword 2 Answer Key

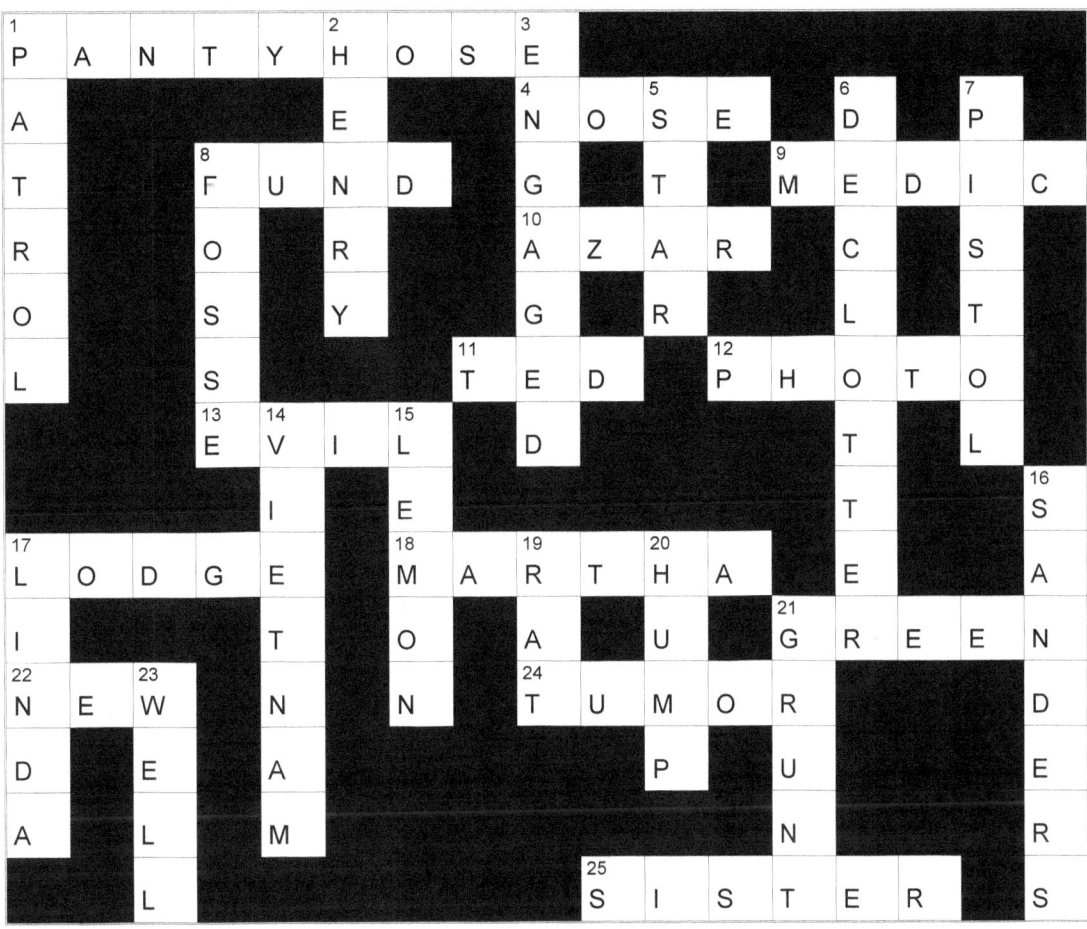

Across
1. Good-luck item for Dobbins
4. Jensen broke his own
8. Note with money in envelope said Emergency ___.
9. Jorgenson's job
10. Aids O'Brien in getting revenge
11. Escapes the realities of the war by using drugs
12. It indirectly causes Kiowa's death.
13. Narrator found it difficult to admit he was capable of this.
17. Narrator drove to the Tip Top ___
18. Lt. Cross burned her picture
21. The ___ Berets used the compound as their base.
22. Kiowa received an illustrated ___ Testament.
24. Cause of Linda's demise
25. Rat wrote to Curt Lemon's

Down
1. The listening ___ heard sounds foreign to the jungle.
2. His girlfriend dumped him in October; monks liked him
3. Mark compromised with Mary Anne and they became ___.
5. Shape of the Vietnamese soldier's wound
6. O'Brien's summer job in 1968
7. Object that broke Jensen's nose
8. Brought his girlfriend to Vietnam for a visit
14. Country & name of the war
15. Fainted during a dentist visit
16. Confessed he made up parts of the story
17. Fourth-grade girlfriend of O'Brien
19. Known for exaggerating
20. To carry
21. Any soldier
23. Dobbins threatens to put Azar in one.

# The Things They Carried Crossword 3

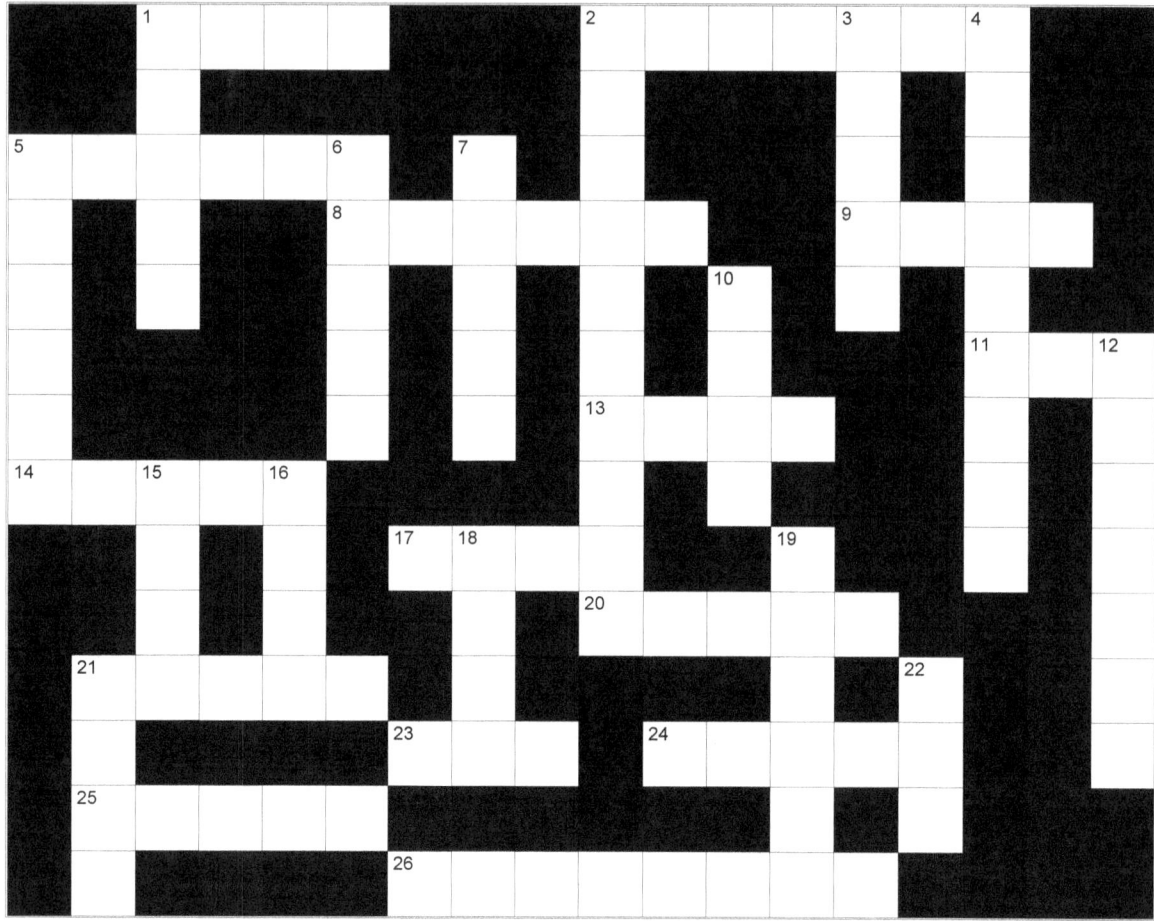

**Across**
1. Kiley shot himself there.
2. To get killed
5. Object that broke Jensen's nose
8. Believes that stories can save lives
9. Dobbins threatens to put Azar in one.
11. Escapes the realities of the war by using drugs
13. Narrator found it difficult to admit he was capable of this.
14. Fourth-grade girlfriend of O'Brien
17. Shape of the Vietnamese soldier's wound
20. Cause of Linda's demise
21. His girlfriend dumped him in October; monks liked him
23. Kiowa received an illustrated ___ Testament.
24. Name of the Company
25. Jorgenson's job
26. Kiowa advised soldiers not to damage or profane these.

**Down**
1. Brought his girlfriend to Vietnam for a visit
2. Mary Anne was the ___ of the Song Tra Bong.
3. Native American soldier
4. O'Brien's summer job in 1968
5. The listening ___ heard sounds foreign to the jungle.
6. Narrator drove to the Tip Top ___
7. The ___ Berets used the compound as their base.
10. Narrator gave Kathleen a ___ to Vietnam as a present.
12. Azar mocked this.
15. Jensen broke his own
16. Aids O'Brien in getting revenge
18. A war story is ____ if it embarrasses the listener.
19. Narrator refused to shake hands with one
21. To carry
22. Known for exaggerating

The Things They Carried Crossword 3 Answer Key

Across
1. Kiley shot himself there.
2. To get killed
5. Object that broke Jensen's nose
8. Believes that stories can save lives
9. Dobbins threatens to put Azar in one.
11. Escapes the realities of the war by using drugs
13. Narrator found it difficult to admit he was capable of this.
14. Fourth-grade girlfriend of O'Brien
17. Shape of the Vietnamese soldier's wound
20. Cause of Linda's demise
21. His girlfriend dumped him in October; monks liked him
23. Kiowa received an illustrated ___ Testament.
24. Name of the Company
25. Jorgenson's job
26. Kiowa advised soldiers not to damage or profane these.

Down
1. Brought his girlfriend to Vietnam for a visit
2. Mary Anne was the ___ of the Song Tra Bong.
3. Native American soldier
4. O'Brien's summer job in 1968
5. The listening ___ heard sounds foreign to the jungle.
6. Narrator drove to the Tip Top ___
7. The ___ Berets used the compound as their base.
10. Narrator gave Kathleen a ___ to Vietnam as a present.
12. Azar mocked this.
15. Jensen broke his own
16. Aids O'Brien in getting revenge
18. A war story is ____ if it embarrasses the listener.
19. Narrator refused to shake hands with one
21. To carry
22. Known for exaggerating

# The Things They Carried Crossword 4

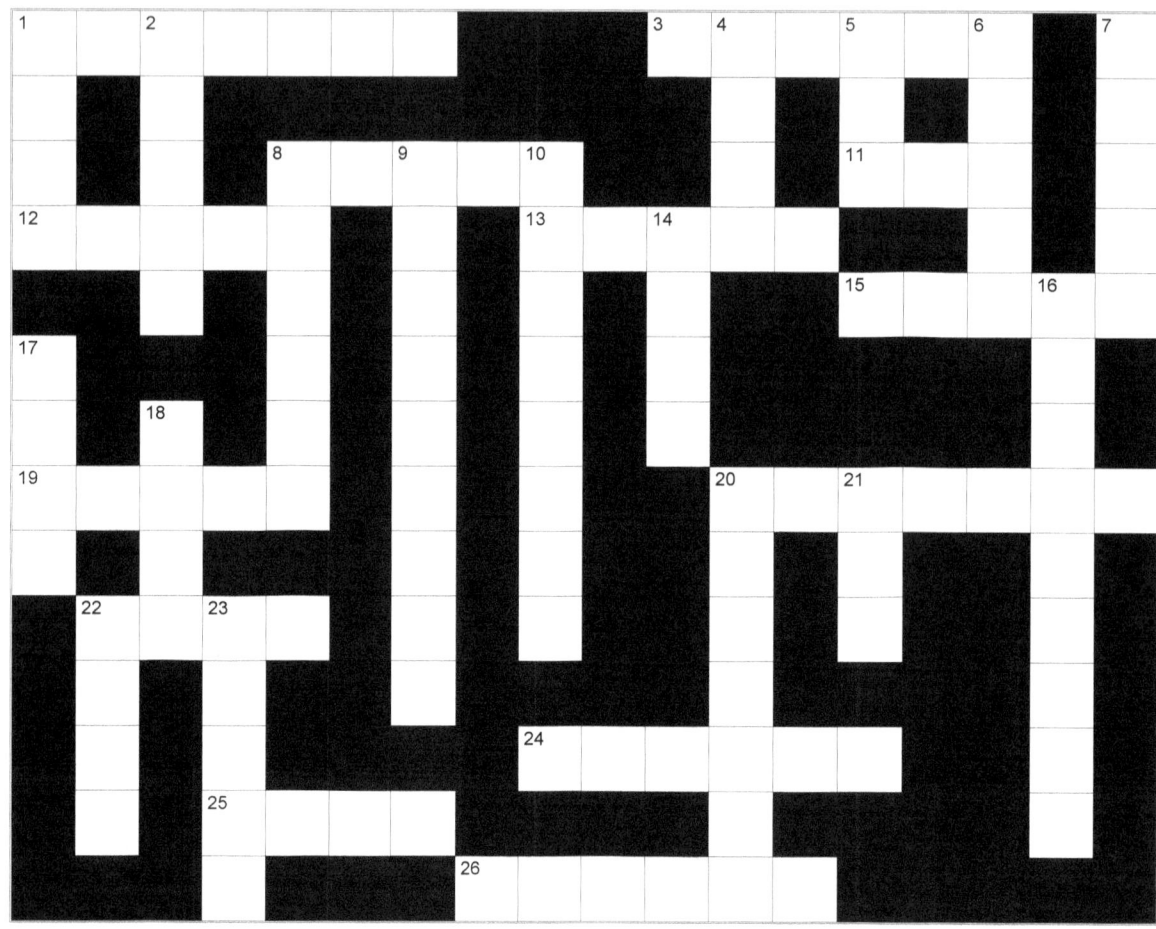

**Across**
1. Mark compromised with Mary Anne and they became ___.
3. The listening ___ heard sounds foreign to the jungle.
8. Jorgenson's job
11. Escapes the realities of the war by using drugs
12. Fourth-grade girlfriend of O'Brien
13. His girlfriend dumped him in October; monks liked him
15. The ___ Berets used the compound as their base.
19. Native American soldier
20. Confessed he made up parts of the story
22. Shape of the Vietnamese soldier's wound
24. Commits suicide
25. To carry
26. Place many draft-dodgers fled to

**Down**
1. Narrator found it difficult to admit he was capable of this.
2. Any soldier
4. Aids O'Brien in getting revenge
5. Known for exaggerating
6. Narrator drove to the Tip Top ___
7. Fainted during a dentist visit
8. Lt. Cross burned her picture
9. O'Brien's summer job in 1968
10. Kiowa advised soldiers not to damage or profane these.
14. Jensen broke his own
16. The muddy field was full of this.
17. Norman drove around it.
18. Kiley shot himself there.
20. To get killed
21. Kiowa received an illustrated ___ Testament.
22. Kiowa ___ into the mud.
23. Name of the Company

# The Things They Carried Crossword 4 Answer Key

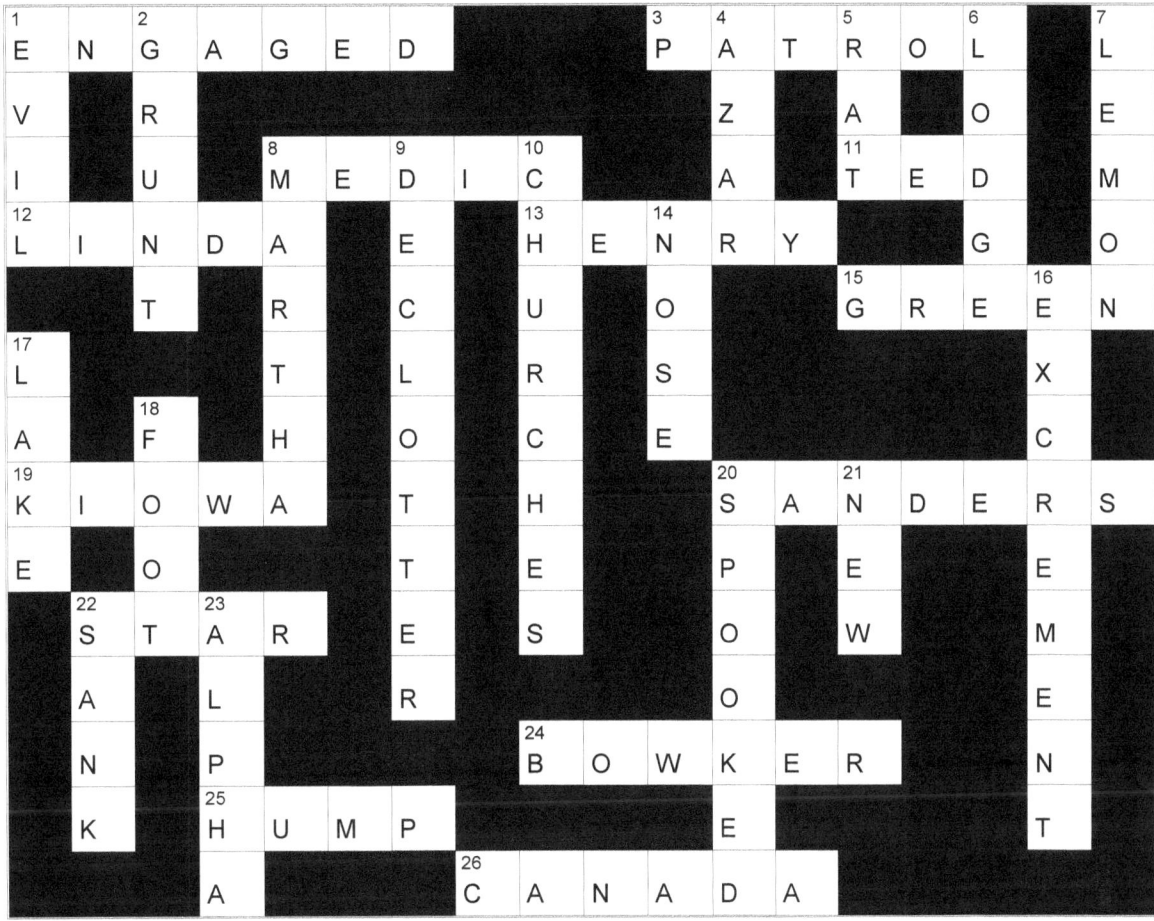

**Across**
1. Mark compromised with Mary Anne and they became ___.
3. The listening ___ heard sounds foreign to the jungle.
8. Jorgenson's job
11. Escapes the realities of the war by using drugs
12. Fourth-grade girlfriend of O'Brien
13. His girlfriend dumped him in October; monks liked him
15. The ___ Berets used the compound as their base.
19. Native American soldier
20. Confessed he made up parts of the story
22. Shape of the Vietnamese soldier's wound
24. Commits suicide
25. To carry
26. Place many draft-dodgers fled to

**Down**
1. Narrator found it difficult to admit he was capable of this.
2. Any soldier
4. Aids O'Brien in getting revenge
5. Known for exaggerating
6. Narrator drove to the Tip Top ___
7. Fainted during a dentist visit
8. Lt. Cross burned her picture
9. O'Brien's summer job in 1968
10. Kiowa advised soldiers not to damage or profane these.
14. Jensen broke his own
16. The muddy field was full of this.
17. Norman drove around it.
18. Kiley shot himself there.
20. To get killed
21. Kiowa received an illustrated ___ Testament.
22. Kiowa ___ into the mud.
23. Name of the Company

The Things They Carried

| TRIP | TRUE | HUMP | CANADA | EXCREMENT |
|---|---|---|---|---|
| KIOWA | LEMON | HENRY | DECLOTTER | SPOOKED |
| STORIES | VIETNAM | FREE SPACE | FOSSE | CORPSE |
| STAR | AZAR | GRUNT | BUFFALO | MEDIC |
| EVIL | WELL | FUND | LINDA | CHURCHES |

The Things They Carried

| LODGE | CARRIED | JACKKNIFE | PANTYHOSE | MOCCASINS |
|---|---|---|---|---|
| LAKE | ENGAGED | SANK | NEW | RAT |
| OBRIEN | TUMOR | FREE SPACE | IRONIC | FOOT |
| COURAGE | ALPHA | NOSE | PHOTO | PATROL |
| BERDAHL | LAVENDER | SANDERS | PISTOL | MARTHA |

The Things They Carried

| BERDAHL | MARTHA | DECLOTTER | IRONIC | FOOT |
|---|---|---|---|---|
| TRUE | WELL | AZAR | ENGAGED | CHURCHES |
| STORIES | STAR | FREE SPACE | CANADA | LODGE |
| LAVENDER | TUMOR | LINDA | JACKKNIFE | TED |
| SWEETHEART | JUNGLE | SANK | PISTOL | DANCING |

The Things They Carried

| RAT | BOWKER | TRIP | EXCREMENT | NEW |
|---|---|---|---|---|
| HUMP | PHOTO | LEMON | PATROL | FOSSE |
| NOSE | HENRY | FREE SPACE | MOCCASINS | KIOWA |
| COURAGE | SPOOKED | SANDERS | MEDIC | ALPHA |
| BUFFALO | EVIL | FUND | OBRIEN | KATHLEEN |

The Things They Carried

| RAT | FOSSE | MARTHA | PHOTO | ALPHA |
|---|---|---|---|---|
| PATROL | NOSE | LODGE | CARRIED | CHURCHES |
| GREEN | SISTER | FREE SPACE | HENRY | JACKKNIFE |
| LEMON | WELL | JUNGLE | BUFFALO | ENGAGED |
| AZAR | DECLOTTER | PANTYHOSE | OBRIEN | TUMOR |

The Things They Carried

| HUMP | SILVER | SANK | SANDERS | PISTOL |
|---|---|---|---|---|
| VIETNAM | CORPSE | COURAGE | DANCING | BOWKER |
| LINDA | FUND | FREE SPACE | BERDAHL | EVIL |
| STORIES | TRIP | SPOOKED | SWEETHEART | LAKE |
| MOCCASINS | EXCREMENT | IRONIC | GRUNT | MEDIC |

## The Things They Carried

| VIETNAM | HENRY | BERDAHL | ALPHA | PANTYHOSE |
|---|---|---|---|---|
| BOWKER | EXCREMENT | CORPSE | KATHLEEN | FUND |
| STAR | DANCING | FREE SPACE | TED | ENGAGED |
| JUNGLE | PHOTO | WELL | LINDA | CANADA |
| EVIL | CHURCHES | MEDIC | SPOOKED | GRUNT |

## The Things They Carried

| HUMP | FOSSE | COURAGE | RAT | TUMOR |
|---|---|---|---|---|
| KIOWA | CARRIED | NEW | OBRIEN | JACKKNIFE |
| TRUE | DECLOTTER | FREE SPACE | PISTOL | SISTER |
| LODGE | PATROL | MARTHA | LAVENDER | MOCCASINS |
| FOOT | AZAR | SWEETHEART | NOSE | IRONIC |

The Things They Carried

| RAT | STORIES | SWEETHEART | FUND | LAKE |
|---|---|---|---|---|
| FOOT | NEW | EXCREMENT | VIETNAM | MEDIC |
| JUNGLE | EVIL | FREE SPACE | BERDAHL | NOSE |
| TED | SPOOKED | JACKKNIFE | KATHLEEN | KIOWA |
| TRIP | ALPHA | MARTHA | PANTYHOSE | LINDA |

The Things They Carried

| WELL | LEMON | DANCING | HUMP | DECLOTTER |
|---|---|---|---|---|
| HENRY | OBRIEN | PISTOL | GREEN | SISTER |
| CHURCHES | ENGAGED | FREE SPACE | CANADA | FOSSE |
| CARRIED | SILVER | LAVENDER | MOCCASINS | LODGE |
| SANK | PATROL | AZAR | GRUNT | COURAGE |

The Things They Carried

| SANDERS | AZAR | PANTYHOSE | KIOWA | PATROL |
| --- | --- | --- | --- | --- |
| SILVER | JACKKNIFE | KATHLEEN | VIETNAM | FOSSE |
| IRONIC | SWEETHEART | FREE SPACE | SISTER | HENRY |
| CARRIED | PISTOL | HUMP | PHOTO | GREEN |
| WELL | EXCREMENT | SPOOKED | TUMOR | DANCING |

The Things They Carried

| OBRIEN | TRIP | RAT | CANADA | MOCCASINS |
| --- | --- | --- | --- | --- |
| STAR | MEDIC | FOOT | STORIES | LEMON |
| FUND | LODGE | FREE SPACE | JUNGLE | NEW |
| DECLOTTER | ALPHA | GRUNT | TRUE | CHURCHES |
| BERDAHL | NOSE | LAKE | SANK | ENGAGED |

The Things They Carried

| FOOT | DECLOTTER | FOSSE | LEMON | IRONIC |
|---|---|---|---|---|
| KATHLEEN | SANK | SISTER | KIOWA | EVIL |
| SWEETHEART | TRIP | FREE SPACE | LAKE | HUMP |
| ALPHA | HENRY | GREEN | OBRIEN | MOCCASINS |
| VIETNAM | TRUE | TUMOR | LODGE | MEDIC |

The Things They Carried

| STORIES | DANCING | CARRIED | BUFFALO | SILVER |
|---|---|---|---|---|
| STAR | PATROL | FUND | WELL | NEW |
| MARTHA | PISTOL | FREE SPACE | SANDERS | LAVENDER |
| GRUNT | SPOOKED | BERDAHL | RAT | CORPSE |
| TED | AZAR | EXCREMENT | BOWKER | CANADA |

The Things They Carried

| MARTHA | PANTYHOSE | SPOOKED | VIETNAM | CANADA |
|---|---|---|---|---|
| MOCCASINS | STORIES | STAR | SANK | PISTOL |
| ALPHA | OBRIEN | FREE SPACE | KATHLEEN | BERDAHL |
| DECLOTTER | CHURCHES | LAVENDER | SILVER | TRIP |
| LINDA | FOSSE | PHOTO | GREEN | MEDIC |

The Things They Carried

| ENGAGED | NEW | FUND | SWEETHEART | JACKKNIFE |
|---|---|---|---|---|
| EXCREMENT | COURAGE | WELL | SISTER | GRUNT |
| LODGE | AZAR | FREE SPACE | DANCING | CORPSE |
| PATROL | LAKE | CARRIED | NOSE | FOOT |
| HUMP | BUFFALO | TED | IRONIC | TUMOR |

The Things They Carried

| STORIES | CANADA | VIETNAM | GRUNT | WELL |
|---------|--------|---------|-------|------|
| DANCING | HENRY | SANK | SISTER | RAT |
| STAR | COURAGE | FREE SPACE | CHURCHES | LEMON |
| JACKKNIFE | GREEN | EVIL | OBRIEN | JUNGLE |
| NOSE | DECLOTTER | ALPHA | KATHLEEN | CARRIED |

The Things They Carried

| PATROL | LINDA | EXCREMENT | AZAR | HUMP |
|--------|-------|-----------|------|------|
| BERDAHL | IRONIC | SANDERS | PISTOL | TRIP |
| FOSSE | MOCCASINS | FREE SPACE | ENGAGED | SWEETHEART |
| TRUE | TED | MEDIC | SPOOKED | PHOTO |
| FOOT | SILVER | TUMOR | NEW | BUFFALO |

The Things They Carried

| PANTYHOSE | MARTHA | OBRIEN | STAR | SANK |
|---|---|---|---|---|
| FOSSE | NOSE | TED | STORIES | EXCREMENT |
| BUFFALO | GRUNT | FREE SPACE | TUMOR | HENRY |
| FOOT | LODGE | LEMON | FUND | PHOTO |
| TRIP | ALPHA | MEDIC | HUMP | KATHLEEN |

The Things They Carried

| BERDAHL | JUNGLE | LINDA | JACKKNIFE | AZAR |
|---|---|---|---|---|
| RAT | PATROL | SWEETHEART | WELL | IRONIC |
| DANCING | CARRIED | FREE SPACE | LAVENDER | MOCCASINS |
| NEW | ENGAGED | CANADA | KIOWA | COURAGE |
| SISTER | CHURCHES | PISTOL | SPOOKED | SILVER |

The Things They Carried

| SWEETHEART | HUMP | TUMOR | SANK | TRIP |
| --- | --- | --- | --- | --- |
| COURAGE | TRUE | LAKE | MOCCASINS | LODGE |
| LAVENDER | IRONIC | FREE SPACE | PANTYHOSE | VIETNAM |
| OBRIEN | NEW | LINDA | PHOTO | STORIES |
| CORPSE | NOSE | GREEN | AZAR | SPOOKED |

The Things They Carried

| MARTHA | MEDIC | JUNGLE | BOWKER | CHURCHES |
| --- | --- | --- | --- | --- |
| SANDERS | CARRIED | FUND | JACKKNIFE | KATHLEEN |
| DECLOTTER | PISTOL | FREE SPACE | PATROL | CANADA |
| LEMON | SILVER | BUFFALO | BERDAHL | RAT |
| EVIL | EXCREMENT | ENGAGED | FOOT | ALPHA |

The Things They Carried

| COURAGE | FOOT | SILVER | LODGE | PANTYHOSE |
|---|---|---|---|---|
| MARTHA | CANADA | SPOOKED | ALPHA | KIOWA |
| MOCCASINS | BERDAHL | FREE SPACE | CHURCHES | AZAR |
| TUMOR | BUFFALO | HENRY | RAT | EVIL |
| KATHLEEN | ENGAGED | PHOTO | LAVENDER | IRONIC |

The Things They Carried

| CORPSE | SISTER | STORIES | LAKE | JUNGLE |
|---|---|---|---|---|
| SANDERS | OBRIEN | EXCREMENT | SWEETHEART | GRUNT |
| HUMP | FOSSE | FREE SPACE | MEDIC | WELL |
| DECLOTTER | CARRIED | GREEN | PATROL | BOWKER |
| TRUE | STAR | LINDA | NEW | DANCING |

The Things They Carried

| WELL | MEDIC | JUNGLE | FUND | LINDA |
|------|-------|--------|------|-------|
| JACKKNIFE | RAT | LEMON | VIETNAM | PANTYHOSE |
| TRIP | HUMP | FREE SPACE | FOSSE | LODGE |
| CARRIED | STORIES | FOOT | CORPSE | IRONIC |
| ENGAGED | ALPHA | TRUE | SANDERS | DECLOTTER |

The Things They Carried

| CANADA | EXCREMENT | KATHLEEN | OBRIEN | BERDAHL |
|--------|-----------|----------|--------|---------|
| NOSE | KIOWA | BOWKER | LAKE | EVIL |
| CHURCHES | SISTER | FREE SPACE | COURAGE | SILVER |
| GRUNT | PATROL | DANCING | TED | MARTHA |
| PHOTO | PISTOL | MOCCASINS | HENRY | TUMOR |

The Things They Carried

| EXCREMENT | JACKKNIFE | CORPSE | LEMON | MARTHA |
|---|---|---|---|---|
| MOCCASINS | ENGAGED | OBRIEN | BUFFALO | ALPHA |
| WELL | DECLOTTER | FREE SPACE | JUNGLE | GREEN |
| LAVENDER | AZAR | GRUNT | HUMP | TRIP |
| SILVER | SISTER | HENRY | STORIES | VIETNAM |

The Things They Carried

| TUMOR | PANTYHOSE | LINDA | BOWKER | COURAGE |
|---|---|---|---|---|
| LODGE | SWEETHEART | BERDAHL | TED | PHOTO |
| KIOWA | PATROL | FREE SPACE | NEW | FUND |
| EVIL | KATHLEEN | CARRIED | STAR | RAT |
| MEDIC | TRUE | DANCING | FOOT | LAKE |

## The Things They Carried

| | | | | |
|---|---|---|---|---|
| EXCREMENT | IRONIC | GREEN | DANCING | VIETNAM |
| JUNGLE | GRUNT | HUMP | MARTHA | HENRY |
| ALPHA | SISTER | FREE SPACE | FUND | PHOTO |
| LAKE | BOWKER | PATROL | OBRIEN | SPOOKED |
| KIOWA | SWEETHEART | MOCCASINS | SILVER | LAVENDER |

## The Things They Carried

| | | | | |
|---|---|---|---|---|
| COURAGE | RAT | NEW | PISTOL | PANTYHOSE |
| MEDIC | AZAR | JACKKNIFE | TED | LEMON |
| DECLOTTER | CHURCHES | FREE SPACE | NOSE | TUMOR |
| BERDAHL | TRIP | ENGAGED | CANADA | BUFFALO |
| TRUE | FOOT | STORIES | EVIL | LODGE |

The Things They Carried

| STAR | DECLOTTER | OBRIEN | GRUNT | EXCREMENT |
| --- | --- | --- | --- | --- |
| PHOTO | AZAR | JUNGLE | LODGE | CORPSE |
| LINDA | SILVER | FREE SPACE | TUMOR | VIETNAM |
| CARRIED | SANK | IRONIC | ENGAGED | MOCCASINS |
| SISTER | KIOWA | MARTHA | DANCING | NOSE |

The Things They Carried

| SPOOKED | TRUE | STORIES | EVIL | PISTOL |
| --- | --- | --- | --- | --- |
| LEMON | BOWKER | TRIP | SWEETHEART | CHURCHES |
| RAT | JACKKNIFE | FREE SPACE | FUND | HENRY |
| HUMP | FOOT | MEDIC | GREEN | FOSSE |
| KATHLEEN | ALPHA | PATROL | PANTYHOSE | SANDERS |

## Things They Carried Vocabulary Word List

| No. | Word | Clue/Definition |
|---|---|---|
| 1. | ACQUIESCENCE | Consent by giving in |
| 2. | AESTHETIC | Concerning the appreciation of beauty or good taste |
| 3. | AFFLUENT | Wealthy |
| 4. | AMBUSH | Sudden attack made from a concealed position |
| 5. | AMORTIZING | Liquidating (a debt, such as a mortgage) |
| 6. | ATROCITY | Appalling act, situation, or thing |
| 7. | BANDOLIER | Pocketed belt for holding ammunition |
| 8. | BARRAGE | Overwhelming, concentrated outpouring |
| 9. | BEDLAM | Noisy uproar and confusion |
| 10. | BIVOUACKED | Camped in a temporary encampment, often in an unsheltered area |
| 11. | BLATANT | Openly obvious |
| 12. | BLUNT | Direct; to the point |
| 13. | CADRE | Group of trained personnel |
| 14. | CATHARSIS | Purifying or figurative cleansing of the emotions |
| 15. | CAUSATION | The order that makes things happen |
| 16. | CAUSEWAY | Raised roadway, as across water or marshland |
| 17. | CENSURE | Criticize |
| 18. | CLARITY | Quality of being perfectly clear |
| 19. | CLEARANCE | Permission |
| 20. | COMPLICITY | Participation in a crime or wrongdoing |
| 21. | COMPOSURE | Quality of being calm and even-tempered |
| 22. | CONCORD | Harmony; agreement of interests or feeling |
| 23. | CONVICTIONS | Beliefs; morals; values |
| 24. | COORDINATES | Directions for a location relating to longitude and latitude |
| 25. | COWLICK | Tuft of hair that grows in a different direction |
| 26. | DEFINITIVE | Certain or conclusive |
| 27. | DEVOUT | Displaying reverence or piety |
| 28. | DIKE | Ditch or channel |
| 29. | DYSENTERY | Inflammatory disorder of the lower intestinal tract |
| 30. | EMBODIED | Represented in bodily or material form |
| 31. | EROTIC | Arousing sexual desire |
| 32. | ESSENCE | Indispensable properties that characterize or identify |
| 33. | EVAPORATE | Disappear; vanish |
| 34. | EVISCERATED | Disemboweled; guts removed |
| 35. | EXUBERANCE | Quality of being extravagantly joyful |
| 36. | FATIGUES | Clothing worn by military personnel |
| 37. | FLECKS | Small bits |
| 38. | FLUKE | Something accidentally good or successful |
| 39. | GANGRENE | Decay of tissue due to disease or infection |
| 40. | GAPE | Stare wonderingly or stupidly |
| 41. | GENTRY | People of a noble or wealthy class |
| 42. | GROPE | Reach about uncertainly or to feel one's way |
| 43. | GYROSCOPE | Spinning device which maintains its orientation |
| 44. | HAMLET | Village |
| 45. | IMMENSE | Grand; large |
| 46. | IMPERATIVE | Necessary; impossible to deter or evade |
| 47. | IMPLACABLE | Impossible to please or appease |
| 48. | INFATUATION | Foolish, unreasoning, or extravagant passion or attraction |
| 49. | INVULNERABLE | Impossible to damage, injure, or wound |
| 50. | KILTER | Good condition or proper form |

**Things They Carried Vocabulary Word List Continued**

| No. | Word | Clue/Definition |
|---|---|---|
| 51. | LATRINE | Rudimentary communal toilet used in a camp or barracks |
| 52. | LAXITY | State of slack, negligence, or carelessness |
| 53. | LEVITATE | Rise in the air and float |
| 54. | LUCID | Easily understood; intelligible |
| 55. | MENACING | Threatening |
| 56. | MUNDANE | Ordinary; common |
| 57. | OBJECTIFY | Regard in an impersonal way |
| 58. | OPAQUE | Does not allow light to pass through |
| 59. | ORDNANCE | Military equipment such as ammunition |
| 60. | PAGODA | Buddhist tower erected as a monument or shrine |
| 61. | PHOSPHORESCENT | Glowing |
| 62. | PIASTER | Basic Monetary unit of South Vietnam |
| 63. | PIOUS | Showing reverence |
| 64. | PLATITUDE | Unoriginal remark |
| 65. | PLODDING | Moving or walking laboriously |
| 66. | POISE | State of being balanced |
| 67. | PROFOUND | Penetrating beyond what is superficial or obvious |
| 68. | PUFFERY | Flattering, often exaggerated praise and publicity |
| 69. | QUAINT | Charmingly odd |
| 70. | RAPPORT | Relationship with mutual trust or caring |
| 71. | RAPTURE | State of being transported by a lofty emotion; ecstasy |
| 72. | RECTITUDE | Moral righteousness |
| 73. | REPROACHED | Charged oneself with blame or a mistake |
| 74. | RETICENCE | Reserve; reluctance |
| 75. | SKEPTIC | One who does not believe an idea |
| 76. | SKEWED | Turned or placed at an angle |
| 77. | SKITTISH | Restlessly active or nervous |
| 78. | SPECULATION | Guessing based on facts; conclusion or opinion reached by conjecture |
| 79. | SPIN | An interpretation |
| 80. | SUPERLATIVES | Things of the highest excellence |
| 81. | SWABS | Cleaning rod or stick with fabric at the end |
| 82. | TANGIBLE | Real or concrete |
| 83. | TAUT | Pulled or drawn tight |
| 84. | TOPOGRAPHY | Description of a place's terrain |
| 85. | TRANSLUCENT | Partially see-through |
| 86. | UNENCUMBERED | Not carrying a burden |
| 87. | VOLITION | Power of choosing; the will |
| 88. | VOUCH | Substantiate by supplying evidence |
| 89. | VULGAR | Indecent |

Copyrighted

Things They Carried Vocabulary Fill In The Blanks 1

1. Small bits
2. Noisy uproar and confusion
3. Reach about uncertainly or to feel one's way
4. Overwhelming, concentrated outpouring
5. Good condition or proper form
6. Necessary; impossible to deter or evade
7. Village
8. Impossible to please or appease
9. Cleaning rod or stick with fabric at the end
10. Ordinary; common
11. Not carrying a burden
12. Moral righteousness
13. Quality of being perfectly clear
14. Regard in an impersonal way
15. People of a noble or wealthy class
16. Pulled or drawn tight
17. Rudimentary communal toilet used in a camp or barracks
18. State of being balanced
19. Does not allow light to pass through
20. Glowing

Things They Carried Vocabulary Fill In The Blanks 1 Answer Key

| FLECKS | 1. Small bits |
| BEDLAM | 2. Noisy uproar and confusion |
| GROPE | 3. Reach about uncertainly or to feel one's way |
| BARRAGE | 4. Overwhelming, concentrated outpouring |
| KILTER | 5. Good condition or proper form |
| IMPERATIVE | 6. Necessary; impossible to deter or evade |
| HAMLET | 7. Village |
| IMPLACABLE | 8. Impossible to please or appease |
| SWABS | 9. Cleaning rod or stick with fabric at the end |
| MUNDANE | 10. Ordinary; common |
| UNENCUMBERED | 11. Not carrying a burden |
| RECTITUDE | 12. Moral righteousness |
| CLARITY | 13. Quality of being perfectly clear |
| OBJECTIFY | 14. Regard in an impersonal way |
| GENTRY | 15. People of a noble or wealthy class |
| TAUT | 16. Pulled or drawn tight |
| LATRINE | 17. Rudimentary communal toilet used in a camp or barracks |
| POISE | 18. State of being balanced |
| OPAQUE | 19. Does not allow light to pass through |
| PHOSPHORESCENT | 20. Glowing |

Things They Carried Vocabulary Fill In The Blanks 2

1. Overwhelming, concentrated outpouring
2. Cleaning rod or stick with fabric at the end
3. Purifying or figurative cleansing of the emotions
4. Stare wonderingly or stupidly
5. Unoriginal remark
6. Ditch or channel
7. Turned or placed at an angle
8. Impossible to damage, injure, or wound
9. Basic monetary unit of South Vietnam
10. Clothing worn by military personnel
11. Necessary; impossible to deter or evade
12. Concerning the appreciation of beauty or good taste
13. Certain or conclusive
14. Charged oneself with blame or a mistake
15. Direct; to the point
16. Relationship with mutual trust or caring
17. Guessing based on facts; conclusion or opinion reached by conjecture
18. Indispensable properties that characterize or identify
19. Substantiate by supplying evidence
20. State of being balanced

Things They Carried Vocabulary Fill In The Blanks 2 Answer Key

| | |
|---|---|
| BARRAGE | 1. Overwhelming, concentrated outpouring |
| SWABS | 2. Cleaning rod or stick with fabric at the end |
| CATHARSIS | 3. Purifying or figurative cleansing of the emotions |
| GAPE | 4. Stare wonderingly or stupidly |
| PLATITUDE | 5. Unoriginal remark |
| DIKE | 6. Ditch or channel |
| SKEWED | 7. Turned or placed at an angle |
| INVULNERABLE | 8. Impossible to damage, injure, or wound |
| PIASTER | 9. Basic monetary unit of South Vietnam |
| FATIGUES | 10. Clothing worn by military personnel |
| IMPERATIVE | 11. Necessary; impossible to deter or evade |
| AESTHETIC | 12. Concerning the appreciation of beauty or good taste |
| DEFINITIVE | 13. Certain or conclusive |
| REPROACHED | 14. Charged oneself with blame or a mistake |
| BLUNT | 15. Direct; to the point |
| RAPPORT | 16. Relationship with mutual trust or caring |
| SPECULATION | 17. Guessing based on facts; conclusion or opinion reached by conjecture |
| ESSENCE | 18. Indispensable properties that characterize or identify |
| VOUCH | 19. Substantiate by supplying evidence |
| POISE | 20. State of being balanced |

Things They Carried Vocabulary Fill In The Blanks 3

_____ 1. Charmingly odd

_____ 2. Substantiate by supplying evidence

_____ 3. Rise in the air and float

_____ 4. Ditch or channel

_____ 5. Directions for a location relating to longitude and latitude

_____ 6. Partially see-through

_____ 7. Criticize

_____ 8. Regard in an impersonal way

_____ 9. Easily understood; intelligible

_____ 10. Moving or walking laboriously

_____ 11. Inflammatory disorder of the lower intestinal tract

_____ 12. Basic monetary unit of South Vietnam

_____ 13. Direct; to the point

_____ 14. Permission

_____ 15. Does not allow light to pass through

_____ 16. An interpretation

_____ 17. Restlessly active or nervous

_____ 18. Small bits

_____ 19. Wealthy

_____ 20. Village

Things They Carried Vocabulary Fill In The Blanks 3 Answer Key

| QUAINT | 1. Charmingly odd |
| VOUCH | 2. Substantiate by supplying evidence |
| LEVITATE | 3. Rise in the air and float |
| DIKE | 4. Ditch or channel |
| COORDINATES | 5. Directions for a location relating to longitude and latitude |
| TRANSLUCENT | 6. Partially see-through |
| CENSURE | 7. Criticize |
| OBJECTIFY | 8. Regard in an impersonal way |
| LUCID | 9. Easily understood; intelligible |
| PLODDING | 10. Moving or walking laboriously |
| DYSENTERY | 11. Inflammatory disorder of the lower intestinal tract |
| PIASTER | 12. Basic monetary unit of South Vietnam |
| BLUNT | 13. Direct; to the point |
| CLEARANCE | 14. Permission |
| OPAQUE | 15. Does not allow light to pass through |
| SPIN | 16. An interpretation |
| SKITTISH | 17. Restlessly active or nervous |
| FLECKS | 18. Small bits |
| AFFLUENT | 19. Wealthy |
| HAMLET | 20. Village |

Things They Carried Vocabulary Fill In The Blanks 4

_____  1. Pulled or drawn tight

_____  2. Spinning device which maintains its orientation

_____  3. Purifying or figurative cleansing of the emotions

_____  4. Glowing

_____  5. Quality of being perfectly clear

_____  6. An interpretation

_____  7. Camped in a temporary encampment, often in an unsheltered area

_____  8. Raised roadway, as across water or marshland

_____  9. Displaying reverence or piety

_____  10. Beliefs; morals; values

_____  11. State of slack, negligence, or carelessness

_____  12. Something accidentally good or successful

_____  13. Foolish, unreasoning, or extravagant passion or attraction

_____  14. Group of trained personnel

_____  15. Rudimentary communal toilet used in a camp or barracks

_____  16. Direct; to the point

_____  17. Disappear; vanish

_____  18. Reach about uncertainly or to feel one's way

_____  19. Small bits

_____  20. Turned or placed at an angle

Things They Carried Vocabulary Fill In The Blanks 4 Answer Key

|  |  |
|---|---|
| TAUT | 1. Pulled or drawn tight |
| GYROSCOPE | 2. Spinning device which maintains its orientation |
| CATHARSIS | 3. Purifying or figurative cleansing of the emotions |
| PHOSPHORESCENT | 4. Glowing |
| CLARITY | 5. Quality of being perfectly clear |
| SPIN | 6. An interpretation |
| BIVOUACKED | 7. Camped in a temporary encampment, often in an unsheltered area |
| CAUSEWAY | 8. Raised roadway, as across water or marshland |
| DEVOUT | 9. Displaying reverence or piety |
| CONVICTIONS | 10. Beliefs; morals; values |
| LAXITY | 11. State of slack, negligence, or carelessness |
| FLUKE | 12. Something accidentally good or successful |
| INFATUATION | 13. Foolish, unreasoning, or extravagant passion or attraction |
| CADRE | 14. Group of trained personnel |
| LATRINE | 15. Rudimentary communal toilet used in a camp or barracks |
| BLUNT | 16. Direct; to the point |
| EVAPORATE | 17. Disappear; vanish |
| GROPE | 18. Reach about uncertainly or to feel one's way |
| FLECKS | 19. Small bits |
| SKEWED | 20. Turned or placed at an angle |

Things They Carried Vocabulary Matching 1

___ 1. OBJECTIFY		A. Noisy uproar and confusion
___ 2. AMORTIZING		B. Appalling act, situation, or thing
___ 3. POISE			C. Regard in an impersonal way
___ 4. RECTITUDE		D. Moral righteousness
___ 5. TOPOGRAPHY		E. Power of choosing; the will
___ 6. DEFINITIVE		F. Showing reverence
___ 7. ATROCITY		G. Ordinary; common
___ 8. ORDNANCE		H. Indecent
___ 9. VOLITION		I. Glowing
___10. SUPERLATIVES		J. Unoriginal remark
___11. PAGODA			K. Flattering, often exaggerated praise and publicity
___12. CLEARANCE		L. Clothing worn by military personnel
___13. PHOSPHORESCENT	M. Description of a place's terrain
___14. VULGAR			N. Indispensable properties that characterize or identify
___15. ESSENCE		O. Buddhist tower erected as a monument or shrine
___16. PUFFERY		P. Certain or conclusive
___17. PLATITUDE		Q. Liquidating (a debt, such as a mortgage)
___18. GANGRENE		R. State of slack, negligence, or carelessness
___19. MUNDANE		S. Permission
___20. LAXITY			T. State of being balanced
___21. AESTHETIC		U. Decay of tissue due to disease or infection
___22. PIOUS			V. Things of the highest excellence
___23. CONCORD		W. Concerning the appreciation of beauty or good taste
___24. FATIGUES		X. Military equipment such as ammunition
___25. BEDLAM			Y. Harmony; agreement of interests or feeling

Things They Carried Vocabulary Matching 1 Answer Key

| | | |
|---|---|---|
| C - 1. OBJECTIFY | | A. Noisy uproar and confusion |
| Q - 2. AMORTIZING | | B. Appalling act, situation, or thing |
| T - 3. POISE | | C. Regard in an impersonal way |
| D - 4. RECTITUDE | | D. Moral righteousness |
| M - 5. TOPOGRAPHY | | E. Power of choosing; the will |
| P - 6. DEFINITIVE | | F. Showing reverence |
| B - 7. ATROCITY | | G. Ordinary; common |
| X - 8. ORDNANCE | | H. Indecent |
| E - 9. VOLITION | | I. Glowing |
| V - 10. SUPERLATIVES | | J. Unoriginal remark |
| O - 11. PAGODA | | K. Flattering, often exaggerated praise and publicity |
| S - 12. CLEARANCE | | L. Clothing worn by military personnel |
| I - 13. PHOSPHORESCENT | | M. Description of a place's terrain |
| H - 14. VULGAR | | N. Indispensable properties that characterize or identify |
| N - 15. ESSENCE | | O. Buddhist tower erected as a monument or shrine |
| K - 16. PUFFERY | | P. Certain or conclusive |
| J - 17. PLATITUDE | | Q. Liquidating (a debt, such as a mortgage) |
| U - 18. GANGRENE | | R. State of slack, negligence, or carelessness |
| G - 19. MUNDANE | | S. Permission |
| R - 20. LAXITY | | T. State of being balanced |
| W - 21. AESTHETIC | | U. Decay of tissue due to disease or infection |
| F - 22. PIOUS | | V. Things of the highest excellence |
| Y - 23. CONCORD | | W. Concerning the appreciation of beauty or good taste |
| L - 24. FATIGUES | | X. Military equipment such as ammunition |
| A - 25. BEDLAM | | Y. Harmony; agreement of interests or feeling |

Things They Carried Vocabulary Matching 2

___ 1. CENSURE           A. Criticize
___ 2. PUFFERY           B. Showing reverence
___ 3. INVULNERABLE      C. Impossible to damage, injure, or wound
___ 4. PIOUS             D. Direct; to the point
___ 5. QUAINT            E. Camped in a temporary encampment, often in an unsheltered area
___ 6. RAPTURE           F. Real or concrete
___ 7. EVISCERATED       G. Foolish, unreasoning, or extravagant passion or attraction
___ 8. COMPOSURE         H. Disemboweled; guts removed
___ 9. INFATUATION       I. Necessary; impossible to deter or evade
___ 10. CLARITY          J. Power of choosing; the will
___ 11. IMPERATIVE       K. Grand; large
___ 12. COWLICK          L. Quality of being calm and even-tempered
___ 13. BLUNT            M. Represented in bodily or material form
___ 14. TANGIBLE         N. Basic monetary unit of South Vietnam
___ 15. SPIN             O. Overwhelming, concentrated outpouring
___ 16. BIVOUACKED       P. Quality of being perfectly clear
___ 17. BARRAGE          Q. Participation in a crime or wrongdoing
___ 18. IMMENSE          R. Partially see-through
___ 19. COMPLICITY       S. Tuft of hair that grows in a different direction
___ 20. TRANSLUCENT      T. An interpretation
___ 21. EMBODIED         U. State of being transported by a lofty emotion; ecstasy
___ 22. GENTRY           V. People of a noble or wealthy class
___ 23. CONCORD          W. Harmony; agreement of interests or feeling
___ 24. VOLITION         X. Flattering, often exaggerated praise and publicity
___ 25. PIASTER          Y. Charmingly odd

Things They Carried Vocabulary Matching 2 Answer Key

| | | |
|---|---|---|
| A - 1. CENSURE | A. | Criticize |
| X - 2. PUFFERY | B. | Showing reverence |
| C - 3. INVULNERABLE | C. | Impossible to damage, injure, or wound |
| B - 4. PIOUS | D. | Direct; to the point |
| Y - 5. QUAINT | E. | Camped in a temporary encampment, often in an unsheltered area |
| U - 6. RAPTURE | F. | Real or concrete |
| H - 7. EVISCERATED | G. | Foolish, unreasoning, or extravagant passion or attraction |
| L - 8. COMPOSURE | H. | Disemboweled; guts removed |
| G - 9. INFATUATION | I. | Necessary; impossible to deter or evade |
| P - 10. CLARITY | J. | Power of choosing; the will |
| I - 11. IMPERATIVE | K. | Grand; large |
| S - 12. COWLICK | L. | Quality of being calm and even-tempered |
| D - 13. BLUNT | M. | Represented in bodily or material form |
| F - 14. TANGIBLE | N. | Basic monetary unit of South Vietnam |
| T - 15. SPIN | O. | Overwhelming, concentrated outpouring |
| E - 16. BIVOUACKED | P. | Quality of being perfectly clear |
| O - 17. BARRAGE | Q. | Participation in a crime or wrongdoing |
| K - 18. IMMENSE | R. | Partially see-through |
| Q - 19. COMPLICITY | S. | Tuft of hair that grows in a different direction |
| R - 20. TRANSLUCENT | T. | An interpretation |
| M - 21. EMBODIED | U. | State of being transported by a lofty emotion; ecstasy |
| V - 22. GENTRY | V. | People of a noble or wealthy class |
| W - 23. CONCORD | W. | Harmony; agreement of interests or feeling |
| J - 24. VOLITION | X. | Flattering, often exaggerated praise and publicity |
| N - 25. PIASTER | Y. | Charmingly odd |

Things They Carried Vocabulary Matching 3

___ 1. MUNDANE
___ 2. AMORTIZING
___ 3. SUPERLATIVES
___ 4. EXUBERANCE
___ 5. AFFLUENT
___ 6. CLARITY
___ 7. BANDOLIER
___ 8. GYROSCOPE
___ 9. INFATUATION
___ 10. CONVICTIONS
___ 11. DEFINITIVE
___ 12. CONCORD
___ 13. PROFOUND
___ 14. INVULNERABLE
___ 15. CATHARSIS
___ 16. QUAINT
___ 17. AMBUSH
___ 18. HAMLET
___ 19. SKITTISH
___ 20. CAUSEWAY
___ 21. TANGIBLE
___ 22. EVAPORATE
___ 23. DIKE
___ 24. ORDNANCE
___ 25. UNENCUMBERED

A. Quality of being extravagantly joyful
B. Pocketed belt for holding ammunition
C. Charmingly odd
D. Wealthy
E. Spinning device which maintains its orientation
F. Village
G. Liquidating (a debt, such as a mortgage)
H. Harmony; agreement of interests or feeling
I. Impossible to damage, injure, or wound
J. Ordinary; common
K. Quality of being perfectly clear
L. Military equipment such as ammunition
M. Restlessly active or nervous
N. Things of the highest excellence
O. Not carrying a burden
P. Real or concrete
Q. Penetrating beyond what is superficial or obvious
R. Certain or conclusive
S. Raised roadway, as across water or marshland
T. Sudden attack made from a concealed position
U. Purifying or figurative cleansing of the emotions
V. Beliefs; morals; values
W. Foolish, unreasoning, or extravagant passion or attraction
X. Disappear; vanish
Y. Ditch or channel

Things They Carried Vocabulary Matching 3 Answer Key

| | | |
|---|---|---|
| J - 1. MUNDANE | | A. Quality of being extravagantly joyful |
| G - 2. AMORTIZING | | B. Pocketed belt for holding ammunition |
| N - 3. SUPERLATIVES | | C. Charmingly odd |
| A - 4. EXUBERANCE | | D. Wealthy |
| D - 5. AFFLUENT | | E. Spinning device which maintains its orientation |
| K - 6. CLARITY | | F. Village |
| B - 7. BANDOLIER | | G. Liquidating (a debt, such as a mortgage) |
| E - 8. GYROSCOPE | | H. Harmony; agreement of interests or feeling |
| W - 9. INFATUATION | | I. Impossible to damage, injure, or wound |
| V - 10. CONVICTIONS | | J. Ordinary; common |
| R - 11. DEFINITIVE | | K. Quality of being perfectly clear |
| H - 12. CONCORD | | L. Military equipment such as ammunition |
| Q - 13. PROFOUND | | M. Restlessly active or nervous |
| I - 14. INVULNERABLE | | N. Things of the highest excellence |
| U - 15. CATHARSIS | | O. Not carrying a burden |
| C - 16. QUAINT | | P. Real or concrete |
| T - 17. AMBUSH | | Q. Penetrating beyond what is superficial or obvious |
| F - 18. HAMLET | | R. Certain or conclusive |
| M - 19. SKITTISH | | S. Raised roadway, as across water or marshland |
| S - 20. CAUSEWAY | | T. Sudden attack made from a concealed position |
| P - 21. TANGIBLE | | U. Purifying or figurative cleansing of the emotions |
| X - 22. EVAPORATE | | V. Beliefs; morals; values |
| Y - 23. DIKE | | W. Foolish, unreasoning, or extravagant passion or attraction |
| L - 24. ORDNANCE | | X. Disappear; vanish |
| O - 25. UNENCUMBERED | | Y. Ditch or channel |

Things They Carried Vocabulary Matching 4

___ 1. KILTER
___ 2. DEFINITIVE
___ 3. IMMENSE
___ 4. GANGRENE
___ 5. AFFLUENT
___ 6. RETICENCE
___ 7. PUFFERY
___ 8. UNENCUMBERED
___ 9. GYROSCOPE
___10. CATHARSIS
___11. INVULNERABLE
___12. PHOSPHORESCENT
___13. SKEWED
___14. PAGODA
___15. PLATITUDE
___16. BLUNT
___17. PLODDING
___18. EMBODIED
___19. ACQUIESCENCE
___20. SUPERLATIVES
___21. AMORTIZING
___22. CLEARANCE
___23. PROFOUND
___24. VULGAR
___25. GAPE

A. Grand; large
B. Indecent
C. Moving or walking laboriously
D. Glowing
E. Flattering, often exaggerated praise and publicity
F. Stare wonderingly or stupidly
G. Decay of tissue due to disease or infection
H. Consent by giving in
I. Wealthy
J. Permission
K. Represented in bodily or material form
L. Penetrating beyond what is superficial or obvious
M. Liquidating (a debt, such as a mortgage)
N. Good condition or proper form
O. Purifying or figurative cleansing of the emotions
P. Things of the highest excellence
Q. Direct; to the point
R. Reserve; reluctance
S. Unoriginal remark
T. Turned or placed at an angle
U. Impossible to damage, injure, or wound
V. Certain or conclusive
W. Buddhist tower erected as a monument or shrine
X. Spinning device which maintains its orientation
Y. Not carrying a burden

Things They Carried Vocabulary Matching 4 Answer Key

| | | |
|---|---|---|
| N - 1. KILTER | A. | Grand; large |
| V - 2. DEFINITIVE | B. | Indecent |
| A - 3. IMMENSE | C. | Moving or walking laboriously |
| G - 4. GANGRENE | D. | Glowing |
| I - 5. AFFLUENT | E. | Flattering, often exaggerated praise and publicity |
| R - 6. RETICENCE | F. | Stare wonderingly or stupidly |
| E - 7. PUFFERY | G. | Decay of tissue due to disease or infection |
| Y - 8. UNENCUMBERED | H. | Consent by giving in |
| X - 9. GYROSCOPE | I. | Wealthy |
| O - 10. CATHARSIS | J. | Permission |
| U - 11. INVULNERABLE | K. | Represented in bodily or material form |
| D - 12. PHOSPHORESCENT | L. | Penetrating beyond what is superficial or obvious |
| T - 13. SKEWED | M. | Liquidating (a debt, such as a mortgage) |
| W - 14. PAGODA | N. | Good condition or proper form |
| S - 15. PLATITUDE | O. | Purifying or figurative cleansing of the emotions |
| Q - 16. BLUNT | P. | Things of the highest excellence |
| C - 17. PLODDING | Q. | Direct; to the point |
| K - 18. EMBODIED | R. | Reserve; reluctance |
| H - 19. ACQUIESCENCE | S. | Unoriginal remark |
| P - 20. SUPERLATIVES | T. | Turned or placed at an angle |
| M - 21. AMORTIZING | U. | Impossible to damage, injure, or wound |
| J - 22. CLEARANCE | V. | Certain or conclusive |
| L - 23. PROFOUND | W. | Buddhist tower erected as a monument or shrine |
| B - 24. VULGAR | X. | Spinning device which maintains its orientation |
| F - 25. GAPE | Y. | Not carrying a burden |

Things They Carried Vocabulary Magic Squares 1

Match the definition with the vocabulary word. Put your answers in the magic squares below. When your answers are correct, all columns and rows will add to the same number.

A. EROTIC
B. HAMLET
C. DIKE
D. MENACING
E. POISE
F. ACQUIESCENCE
G. LEVITATE
H. OPAQUE
I. EXUBERANCE
J. VOUCH
K. RETICENCE
L. PUFFERY
M. PIASTER
N. SPIN
O. DYSENTERY
P. BLATANT

1. Ditch or channel
2. Substantiate by supplying evidence
3. Consent by giving in
4. Inflammatory disorder of the lower intestinal tract
5. Openly obvious
6. State of being balanced
7. Quality of being extravagantly joyful
8. Threatening
9. Basic monetary unit of South Vietnam
10. Does not allow light to pass through
11. Flattering, often exaggerated praise and publicity
12. Arousing sexual desire
13. Village
14. Reserve; reluctance
15. Rise in the air and float
16. An interpretation

| A= | B= | C= | D= |
| --- | --- | --- | --- |
| E= | F= | G= | H= |
| I= | J= | K= | L= |
| M= | N= | O= | P= |

Things They Carried Vocabulary Magic Squares 1 Answer Key

Match the definition with the vocabulary word. Put your answers in the magic squares below. When your answers are correct, all columns and rows will add to the same number.

A. EROTIC
B. HAMLET
C. DIKE
D. MENACING
E. POISE
F. ACQUIESCENCE
G. LEVITATE
H. OPAQUE
I. EXUBERANCE
J. VOUCH
K. RETICENCE
L. PUFFERY
M. PIASTER
N. SPIN
O. DYSENTERY
P. BLATANT

1. Ditch or channel
2. Substantiate by supplying evidence
3. Consent by giving in
4. Inflammatory disorder of the lower intestinal tract
5. Openly obvious
6. State of being balanced
7. Quality of being extravagantly joyful
8. Threatening
9. Basic monetary unit of South Vietnam
10. Does not allow light to pass through
11. Flattering, often exaggerated praise and publicity
12. Arousing sexual desire
13. Village
14. Reserve; reluctance
15. Rise in the air and float
16. An interpretation

| A=12 | B=13 | C=1 | D=8 |
| --- | --- | --- | --- |
| E=6 | F=3 | G=15 | H=10 |
| I=7 | J=2 | K=14 | L=11 |
| M=9 | N=16 | O=4 | P=5 |

Things They Carried Vocabulary Magic Squares 2

Match the definition with the vocabulary word. Put your answers in the magic squares below. When your answers are correct, all columns and rows will add to the same number.

A. COMPLICITY
B. RETICENCE
C. RAPTURE
D. BANDOLIER
E. CAUSATION
F. CONVICTIONS
G. LATRINE
H. CAUSEWAY
I. RECTITUDE
J. COMPOSURE
K. ACQUIESCENCE
L. KILTER
M. CLARITY
N. FLUKE
O. DYSENTERY
P. UNENCUMBERED

1. Inflammatory disorder of the lower intestinal tract
2. Pocketed belt for holding ammunition
3. Quality of being calm and even-tempered
4. The order that makes things happen
5. Moral righteousness
6. Beliefs; morals; values
7. Not carrying a burden
8. State of being transported by a lofty emotion; ecstasy
9. Raised roadway, as across water or marshland
10. Consent by giving in
11. Participation in a crime or wrongdoing
12. Something accidentally good or successful
13. Reserve; reluctance
14. Quality of being perfectly clear
15. Rudimentary communal toilet used in a camp or barracks
16. Good condition or proper form

| | | | |
|---|---|---|---|
| A= | B= | C= | D= |
| E= | F= | G= | H= |
| I= | J= | K= | L= |
| M= | N= | O= | P= |

Things They Carried Vocabulary Magic Squares 2 Answer Key

Match the definition with the vocabulary word. Put your answers in the magic squares below. When your answers are correct, all columns and rows will add to the same number.

A. COMPLICITY
B. RETICENCE
C. RAPTURE
D. BANDOLIER
E. CAUSATION
F. CONVICTIONS
G. LATRINE
H. CAUSEWAY
I. RECTITUDE
J. COMPOSURE
K. ACQUIESCENCE
L. KILTER
M. CLARITY
N. FLUKE
O. DYSENTERY
P. UNENCUMBERED

1. Inflammatory disorder of the lower intestinal tract
2. Pocketed belt for holding ammunition
3. Quality of being calm and even-tempered
4. The order that makes things happen
5. Moral righteousness
6. Beliefs; morals; values
7. Not carrying a burden
8. State of being transported by a lofty emotion; ecstasy
9. Raised roadway, as across water or marshland
10. Consent by giving in
11. Participation in a crime or wrongdoing
12. Something accidentally good or successful
13. Reserve; reluctance
14. Quality of being perfectly clear
15. Rudimentary communal toilet used in a camp or barracks
16. Good condition or proper form

| A=11 | B=13 | C=8 | D=2 |
| --- | --- | --- | --- |
| E=4 | F=6 | G=15 | H=9 |
| I=5 | J=3 | K=10 | L=16 |
| M=14 | N=12 | O=1 | P=7 |

Things They Carried Vocabulary Magic Squares 3

Match the definition with the vocabulary word. Put your answers in the magic squares below. When your answers are correct, all columns and rows will add to the same number.

A. VOLITION
B. QUAINT
C. RETICENCE
D. KILTER
E. DIKE
F. COMPLICITY
G. CAUSEWAY
H. LAXITY
I. PLATITUDE
J. DYSENTERY
K. CLARITY
L. EVAPORATE
M. UNENCUMBERED
N. BLATANT
O. LUCID
P. VULGAR

1. Charmingly odd
2. Raised roadway, as across water or marshland
3. Quality of being perfectly clear
4. Openly obvious
5. Not carrying a burden
6. Disappear; vanish
7. State of slack, negligence, or carelessness
8. Power of choosing; the will
9. Indecent
10. Unoriginal remark
11. Ditch or channel
12. Good condition or proper form
13. Reserve; reluctance
14. Participation in a crime or wrongdoing
15. Inflammatory disorder of the lower intestinal tract
16. Easily understood; intelligible

| A= | B= | C= | D= |
| E= | F= | G= | H= |
| I= | J= | K= | L= |
| M= | N= | O= | P= |

Things They Carried Vocabulary Magic Squares 3 Answer Key

Match the definition with the vocabulary word. Put your answers in the magic squares below. When your answers are correct, all columns and rows will add to the same number.

A. VOLITION
B. QUAINT
C. RETICENCE
D. KILTER
E. DIKE
F. COMPLICITY
G. CAUSEWAY
H. LAXITY
I. PLATITUDE
J. DYSENTERY
K. CLARITY
L. EVAPORATE
M. UNENCUMBERED
N. BLATANT
O. LUCID
P. VULGAR

1. Charmingly odd
2. Raised roadway, as across water or marshland
3. Quality of being perfectly clear
4. Openly obvious
5. Not carrying a burden
6. Disappear; vanish
7. State of slack, negligence, or carelessness
8. Power of choosing; the will
9. Indecent
10. Unoriginal remark
11. Ditch or channel
12. Good condition or proper form
13. Reserve; reluctance
14. Participation in a crime or wrongdoing
15. Inflammatory disorder of the lower intestinal tract
16. Easily understood; intelligible

| A=8 | B=1 | C=13 | D=12 |
| --- | --- | --- | --- |
| E=11 | F=14 | G=2 | H=7 |
| I=10 | J=15 | K=3 | L=6 |
| M=5 | N=4 | O=16 | P=9 |

Things They Carried Vocabulary Magic Squares 4

Match the definition with the vocabulary word. Put your answers in the magic squares below. When your answers are correct, all columns and rows will add to the same number.

A. EVISCERATED
B. DEFINITIVE
C. HAMLET
D. SKEPTIC
E. SWABS
F. RETICENCE
G. LATRINE
H. SKITTISH
I. CLARITY
J. CENSURE
K. KILTER
L. FATIGUES
M. GANGRENE
N. ORDNANCE
O. DEVOUT
P. RAPPORT

1. Disemboweled; guts removed
2. Military equipment such as ammunition
3. Criticize
4. Cleaning rod or stick with fabric at the end
5. Rudimentary communal toilet used in a camp or barracks
6. Clothing worn by military personnel
7. Relationship with mutual trust or caring
8. Village
9. Displaying reverence or piety
10. One who does not believe an idea
11. Restlessly active or nervous
12. Good condition or proper form
13. Quality of being perfectly clear
14. Reserve; reluctance
15. Certain or conclusive
16. Decay of tissue due to disease or infection

| A= | B= | C= | D= |
| E= | F= | G= | H= |
| I= | J= | K= | L= |
| M= | N= | O= | P= |

Things They Carried Vocabulary Magic Squares 4 Answer Key

Match the definition with the vocabulary word. Put your answers in the magic squares below. When your answers are correct, all columns and rows will add to the same number.

A. EVISCERATED
B. DEFINITIVE
C. HAMLET
D. SKEPTIC
E. SWABS
F. RETICENCE
G. LATRINE
H. SKITTISH
I. CLARITY
J. CENSURE
K. KILTER
L. FATIGUES
M. GANGRENE
N. ORDNANCE
O. DEVOUT
P. RAPPORT

1. Disemboweled; guts removed
2. Military equipment such as ammunition
3. Criticize
4. Cleaning rod or stick with fabric at the end
5. Rudimentary communal toilet used in a camp or barracks
6. Clothing worn by military personnel
7. Relationship with mutual trust or caring
8. Village
9. Displaying reverence or piety
10. One who does not believe an idea
11. Restlessly active or nervous
12. Good condition or proper form
13. Quality of being perfectly clear
14. Reserve; reluctance
15. Certain or conclusive
16. Decay of tissue due to disease or infection

| A=1 | B=15 | C=8 | D=10 |
| --- | --- | --- | --- |
| E=4 | F=14 | G=5 | H=11 |
| I=13 | J=3 | K=12 | L=6 |
| M=16 | N=2 | O=9 | P=7 |

Things They Carried Vocabulary Word Search 1

```
T A C E R A P T U R E C A U S A T I O N
H M B V B A R R A G E O L R V O U C H K
A B L A T A N T D A H N P A G O D A F W
M U V P I O U S E N K V V H R C V D T V
L S W O E Y B R V G G I U L G I Y R F B
E H N R C R F L O R W C L U C R T E L Z
T S V A C I O Y U E R T G C M W O Y U P
O B S T H R M T T N C I A I L J D P K M
J P B E D L A M I E T O R D N A N C E R
G O A Z N C Y U E C R N M X T C X N S J
J I T Q M C W N K N K S G P Z Q F I V N
B S N C U Y E D Y P S R Q L L U T C T Y
M E G A P E P A Z I W E X E A I X S A Y
R E Z T C L L N T A A X S V T E C K U P
A K N H O A O E S S B V P I R S F I T P
P I F A N T D Y P T S B I T O C L T T G
P L W R C R D I K E R F N A C E E T F Y
O T K S O I I D P R F V T T I N C I G C
R E C I R N N S K E W E D E T C K S Y R
T R B S D E G G E N T R Y K Y E S H M D
```

An interpretation (4)
Appalling act, situation, or thing (8)
Arousing sexual desire (6)
Beliefs; morals; values (11)
Buddhist tower erected as a monument or shrine (6)
Cleaning rod or stick with fabric at the end (5)
Consent by giving in (12)
Decay of tissue due to disease or infection (8)
Direct; to the point (5)
Disappear; vanish (9)
Displaying reverence or piety (6)
Ditch or channel (4)
Does not allow light to pass through (6)
Easily understood; intelligible (5)
Basic monetary unit of South Vietnam (7)
Good condition or proper form (6)
Grand; large (7)
Group of trained personnel (5)
Harmony; agreement of interests or feeling (7)
Indecent (6)
Indispensable properties that characterize or identify (7)
Military equipment such as ammunition (8)
Moving or walking laboriously (8)
Noisy uproar and confusion (6)
Openly obvious (7)
Ordinary; common (7)

Overwhelming, concentrated outpouring (7)
Participation in a crime or wrongdoing (10)
People of a noble or wealthy class (6)
Pulled or drawn tight (4)
Purifying or figurative cleansing of the emotions (9)
Quality of being perfectly clear (7)
Reach about uncertainty or to feel one's way (5)
Relationship with mutual trust or caring (7)
Restlessly active or nervous (8)
Rise in the air and float (8)
Rudimentary communal toilet used in a camp or barracks (7)
Showing reverence (5)
Small bits (6)
Something accidentally good or successful (5)
Stare wonderingly or stupidly (4)
State of being balanced (5)
State of being transported by a lofty emotion; ecstasy (7)
State of slack, negligence, or carelessness (6)
Substantiate by supplying evidence (5)
Sudden attack made from a concealed position (6)
The order that makes things happen (9)
Threatening (8)
Turned or placed at an angle (6)
Village (6)

Things They Carried Vocabulary Word Search 1 Answer Key

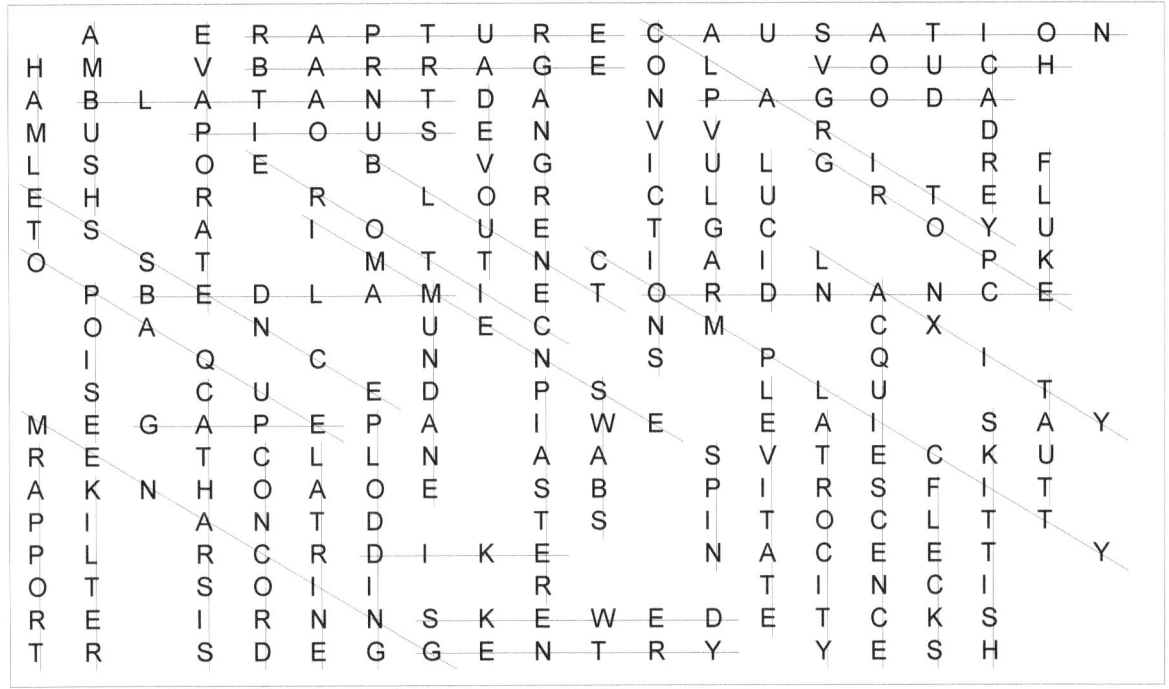

An interpretation (4)
Appalling act, situation, or thing (8)
Arousing sexual desire (6)
Beliefs; morals; values (11)
Buddhist tower erected as a monument or shrine (6)
Cleaning rod or stick with fabric at the end (5)
Consent by giving in (12)
Decay of tissue due to disease or infection (8)
Direct; to the point (5)
Disappear; vanish (9)
Displaying reverence or piety (6)
Ditch or channel (4)
Does not allow light to pass through (6)
Easily understood; intelligible (5)
Basic monetary unit of South Vietnam (7)
Good condition or proper form (6)
Grand; large (7)
Group of trained personnel (5)
Harmony; agreement of interests or feeling (7)
Indecent (6)
Indispensable properties that characterize or identify (7)
Military equipment such as ammunition (8)
Moving or walking laboriously (8)
Noisy uproar and confusion (6)
Openly obvious (7)
Ordinary; common (7)

Overwhelming, concentrated outpouring (7)
Participation in a crime or wrongdoing (10)
People of a noble or wealthy class (6)
Pulled or drawn tight (4)
Purifying or figurative cleansing of the emotions (9)
Quality of being perfectly clear (7)
Reach about uncertainly or to feel one's way (5)
Relationship with mutual trust or caring (7)
Restlessly active or nervous (8)
Rise in the air and float (8)
Rudimentary communal toilet used in a camp or barracks (7)
Showing reverence (5)
Small bits (6)
Something accidentally good or successful (5)
Stare wonderingly or stupidly (4)
State of being balanced (5)
State of being transported by a lofty emotion; ecstasy (7)
State of slack, negligence, or carelessness (6)
Substantiate by supplying evidence (5)
Sudden attack made from a concealed position (6)
The order that makes things happen (9)
Threatening (8)
Turned or placed at an angle (6)
Village (6)

Things They Carried Vocabulary Word Search 2

```
F P U F F E R Y L E V I T A T E D I K E
S L K P A T E E B Q X O N A L R E M L B
V Y E G N T T P P L U U U V U O V M U K
G L Y C D Z I V I R A B C X T O E C H
G A P E K B C G U A O T I E H I U N I T
H X N G G S E B U L S A A N R C T S D K
P I R G Y H N D L E G T C N T A Z E D P
H T A M R L C G L U S A E H T X N C N C
O Y P B O E E C F A N G R R E G P C C Q
S X P Y S C N L V S M T S J V D C R E G
P R O C C A H E T K C Q K Q O P A V M L
H A R A O D A A A I L B E N L O U Y B N
O P T T P R M R N T A S W L I I S B O Z
R T B H E E L A G T R B E A T S E C D D
E U M A B H E N I I I O D T I E W O I V
S R L R R G T C B S T K C R O W A N E S
C E N S U R E E L H Y S P I N N Y C D J
E N V I Q O A G E N T R Y N T Y Q O K N
N V X S S P T G M K I L T E R Y D R B T
T F L U K E S P E C U L A T I O N D Q B
```

An interpretation (4)
Appalling act, situation, or thing (8)
Arousing sexual desire (6)
Charged oneself with blame or a mistake (10)
Charmingly odd (6)
Clothing worn by military personnel (8)
Criticize (7)
Decay of tissue due to disease or infection (8)
Direct; to the point (5)
Displaying reverence or piety (6)
Ditch or channel (4)
Easily understood; intelligible (5)
Flattering, often exaggerated praise and publicity (7)
Basic monetary unit of South Vietnam (7)
Glowing (14)
Good condition or proper form (6)
Grand; large (7)
Group of trained personnel (5)
Guessing based on facts; conclusion or opinion reached by conjecture (11)
Harmony; agreement of interests or feeling (7)
Indecent (6)
Noisy uproar and confusion (6)
Openly obvious (7)
Overwhelming, concentrated outpouring (7)
People of a noble or wealthy class (6)
Permission (9)
Power of choosing; the will (8)
Pulled or drawn tight (4)
Purifying or figurative cleansing of the emotions (9)
Quality of being extravagantly joyful (10)
Quality of being perfectly clear (7)
Raised roadway, as across water or marshland (8)
Reach about uncertainly or to feel one's way (5)
Real or concrete (8)
Relationship with mutual trust or caring (7)
Represented in bodily or material form (8)
Reserve; reluctance (9)
Restlessly active or nervous (8)
Rise in the air and float (8)
Rudimentary communal toilet used in a camp or barracks (7)
Small bits (6)
Something accidentally good or successful (5)
Spinning device which maintains its orientation (9)
Stare wonderingly or stupidly (4)
State of being balanced (5)
State of being transported by a lofty emotion; ecstasy (7)
State of slack, negligence, or carelessness (6)
Substantiate by supplying evidence (5)
Turned or placed at an angle (6)
Village (6)

Things They Carried Vocabulary Word Search 2 Answer Key

```
F  P  U  F  F  E  R  Y  L  E  V  I  T  A  T  E  D  I  K  E
   L        A        E  E  B  Q  X  O     A     R  E  M  L
      E           T  T  P  P  L  U  U  U     U  O  V  M  U
G  L     C           I  V  I  R  A  B  C        T  O  E  C
G  A  P  E  K  B  C  G  U  A  O  T  I  E  H  I  U  N  I
   X  N     G  S  E  B  U  L  S  A  A  N  R  C  T  S  D
P  I  R  G  Y     N  D  L  E  G  T  C  N  T  A     E
H  T  A     R     C     L  U  S  A  E  H  T     N
O  Y  P     O  E  E  C     A  N     R  R  E        C
S     P     S  C  N  L     S  M  T  S     V  D  C     E
P  R  O  C  C  A  H  E  T  K  C     K     O  P  A     M
H  A  R  A  O  D  A  A  A  I  L     E     L  O  U     B
O  P  T  T  P  R  M  R  N  T  A     W  L  I  I  S     O
R  T  B  H  E  E  L  A  G  T  R     E  A  T  S  E  C  D
E  U     A        E  N  I  I  I  O  D  T  I  E  W  O  I
S  R     R  R  G  T  C  B  S  T     C  R  O     A  N  E
C  E  N  S  U  R  E  E  L  H  Y  S  P  I  N     Y  C  D
E     I     O  A  G  E  N  T  R  Y  N  T        O
N     S     P        G     K  I  L  T  E  R  Y     R
T  F  L  U  K  E  S  P  E  C  U  L  A  T  I  O  N  D
```

An interpretation (4)
Appalling act, situation, or thing (8)
Arousing sexual desire (6)
Charged oneself with blame or a mistake (10)
Charmingly odd (6)
Clothing worn by military personnel (8)
Criticize (7)
Decay of tissue due to disease or infection (8)
Direct; to the point (5)
Displaying reverence or piety (6)
Ditch or channel (4)
Easily understood; intelligible (5)
Flattering, often exaggerated praise and publicity (7)
Basic monetary unit of South Vietnam (7)
Glowing (14)
Good condition or proper form (6)
Grand; large (7)
Group of trained personnel (5)
Guessing based on facts; conclusion or opinion reached by conjecture (11)
Harmony; agreement of interests or feeling (7)
Indecent (6)
Noisy uproar and confusion (6)
Openly obvious (7)
Overwhelming, concentrated outpouring (7)
People of a noble or wealthy class (6)
Permission (9)

Power of choosing; the will (8)
Pulled or drawn tight (4)
Purifying or figurative cleansing of the emotions (9)
Quality of being extravagantly joyful (10)
Quality of being perfectly clear (7)
Raised roadway, as across water or marshland (8)
Reach about uncertainly or to feel one's way (5)
Real or concrete (8)
Relationship with mutual trust or caring (7)
Represented in bodily or material form (8)
Reserve; reluctance (9)
Restlessly active or nervous (8)
Rise in the air and float (8)
Rudimentary communal toilet used in a camp or barracks (7)
Small bits (6)
Something accidentally good or successful (5)
Spinning device which maintains its orientation (9)
Stare wonderingly or stupidly (4)
State of being balanced (5)
State of being transported by a lofty emotion; ecstasy (7)
State of slack, negligence, or carelessness (6)
Substantiate by supplying evidence (5)
Turned or placed at an angle (6)
Village (6)

Things They Carried Vocabulary Word Search 3

```
R E V A P O R A T E T A N G I B L E F M
B A G E N T R Y P O P W B S M L G C C R
R A P P O R T W C R L M B G E U A A F R
V R Y T N W X Z E D O R G B N C N U F P
H O E E U V G G R N D F E S A I G S L X
F A U P S R X S O A D J O T C D R E E X
L G M C R S E P T N I Y S U I S E W C W
Y S K L H O E I I C N M U B N C N A K V
E X U B E R A N C E G A P E G D E Y S T
S Z B K V T Z C C A V Y E E V D T N J K
F W L W P B C C H E U U R Z R C A L C C
L P A G O D A O Y E X S L O Z A U F W E
U D T B M P D M C K D K A G S B T M N P
K I A O S H R P B J V C T T A C F I R W
E K N P N R E L G U Y A I P I R O X V Y
C E T A C P O I S E S T V U S O Y P C E
L D K Q O I B C Q S L H E F K B N I E X
A E I U W A E I U K A A S F E L G O N S
R V L E L S D T A E X R S E P U R U S B
I O T P I T L Y I W I S B R T N O S U Q
T U E R C E A Z N E T I T Y I T P T R N
Y T R P K R M J T D Y S H J C K E T E G
```

| AMBUSH | COWLICK | GENTRY | PAGODA | RETICENCE |
| BEDLAM | DEVOUT | GROPE | PIASTER | SKEPTIC |
| BLATANT | DIKE | GYROSCOPE | PIOUS | SKEWED |
| BLUNT | EROTIC | HAMLET | PLODDING | SPIN |
| CADRE | ESSENCE | IMPERATIVE | POISE | SUPERLATIVES |
| CATHARSIS | EVAPORATE | KILTER | PROFOUND | SWABS |
| CAUSATION | EXUBERANCE | LAXITY | PUFFERY | TANGIBLE |
| CAUSEWAY | FLECKS | LUCID | QUAINT | TAUT |
| CENSURE | FLUKE | MENACING | RAPPORT | VOUCH |
| CLARITY | GANGRENE | OPAQUE | RAPTURE | VULGAR |
| COMPLICITY | GAPE | ORDNANCE | REPROACHED | |

Things They Carried Vocabulary Word Search 3 Answer Key

| AMBUSH | COWLICK | GENTRY | PAGODA | RETICENCE |
| BEDLAM | DEVOUT | GROPE | PIASTER | SKEPTIC |
| BLATANT | DIKE | GYROSCOPE | PIOUS | SKEWED |
| BLUNT | EROTIC | HAMLET | PLODDING | SPIN |
| CADRE | ESSENCE | IMPERATIVE | POISE | SUPERLATIVES |
| CATHARSIS | EVAPORATE | KILTER | PROFOUND | SWABS |
| CAUSATION | EXUBERANCE | LAXITY | PUFFERY | TANGIBLE |
| CAUSEWAY | FLECKS | LUCID | QUAINT | TAUT |
| CENSURE | FLUKE | MENACING | RAPPORT | VOUCH |
| CLARITY | GANGRENE | OPAQUE | RAPTURE | VULGAR |
| COMPLICITY | GAPE | ORDNANCE | REPROACHED | |

Things They Carried Vocabulary Word Search 4

```
L E V I T A T E V I S C E R A T E D L Z
L A T R I N E J S C P C A U S A T I O N
C Q X S K I T T I S H C Y T T P Q W V K
G O K I Q U A I N T E E T B H B F S O R
P A W A T R O C I T Y N M X S A S A L J
E R N L M Y B A C O V S C R W R R E I B
U X O G I H C D L P U U R E A R A S T X
F N U F R C Y R A O L R T C B A M T I H
M L E B O E K E R G G E K T S G B H O S
E K E N E U N S I R A V A I G E U E N S
N Q H C C R N E T A R O M T L V S T I R
A I A Q K U A D Y P O U O U X T H I M B
C R M S C S M N L H P C R D M T E C M N
I A L P L X B C Y A H T E S D D R E X
N P E G E C U D E E Q K I V P P I W N Q
G T T H A R T C E R U P Z A I B O K S Q
S U P E R L A T I V E S I P N G L I E P
G R L W A W U T Z D O D N O A F R U S Z
F E J Q N Q T T I T R U G R U G L O N E
O B J E C T I F Y V C T T A L S O U P T
G A P E E P I A S T E R O T I C R D K E
P L O D D I N G W C A U S E W A Y S A E
```

| | | | |
|---|---|---|---|
| AESTHETIC | DEVOUT | IMPERATIVE | PROFOUND |
| AMBUSH | DIKE | KILTER | QUAINT |
| AMORTIZING | EROTIC | LATRINE | RAPTURE |
| ATROCITY | ESSENCE | LAXITY | RECTITUDE |
| BARRAGE | EVAPORATE | LEVITATE | SKITTISH |
| BLUNT | EVISCERATED | LUCID | SPIN |
| CADRE | EXUBERANCE | MENACING | SUPERLATIVES |
| CATHARSIS | FLECKS | OBJECTIFY | SWABS |
| CAUSATION | FLUKE | OPAQUE | TAUT |
| CAUSEWAY | GANGRENE | PAGODA | TOPOGRAPHY |
| CENSURE | GAPE | PIASTER | UNENCUMBERED |
| CLARITY | GROPE | PIOUS | VOLITION |
| CLEARANCE | HAMLET | PLODDING | VOUCH |
| COWLICK | IMMENSE | POISE | VULGAR |

Things They Carried Vocabulary Word Search 4 Answer Key

| AESTHETIC | DEVOUT | IMPERATIVE | PROFOUND |
| AMBUSH | DIKE | KILTER | QUAINT |
| AMORTIZING | EROTIC | LATRINE | RAPTURE |
| ATROCITY | ESSENCE | LAXITY | RECTITUDE |
| BARRAGE | EVAPORATE | LEVITATE | SKITTISH |
| BLUNT | EVISCERATED | LUCID | SPIN |
| CADRE | EXUBERANCE | MENACING | SUPERLATIVES |
| CATHARSIS | FLECKS | OBJECTIFY | SWABS |
| CAUSATION | FLUKE | OPAQUE | TAUT |
| CAUSEWAY | GANGRENE | PAGODA | TOPOGRAPHY |
| CENSURE | GAPE | PIASTER | UNENCUMBERED |
| CLARITY | GROPE | PIOUS | VOLITION |
| CLEARANCE | HAMLET | PLODDING | VOUCH |
| COWLICK | IMMENSE | POISE | VULGAR |

Things They Carried Vocabulary Crossword 1

Across
2. Clothing worn by military personnel
6. Ditch or channel
7. Tuft of hair that grows in a different direction
9. Pulled or drawn tight
11. Good condition or proper form
15. Stare wonderingly or stupidly
16. Direct; to the point
18. Charmingly odd
19. An interpretation
20. Substantiate by supplying evidence
21. Indispensable properties that characterize or identify
22. Reach about uncertainly or to feel one's way
23. Criticize

Down
1. Turned or placed at an angle
2. Something accidentally good or successful
3. Description of a place's terrain
4. People of a noble or wealthy class
5. Restlessly active or nervous
7. Group of trained personnel
8. Necessary; impossible to deter or evade
10. Appalling act, situation, or thing
12. Reserve; reluctance
13. Does not allow light to pass through
14. The order that makes things happen
15. Spinning device which maintains its orientation
16. Overwhelming, concentrated outpouring
17. Showing reverence

Things They Carried Vocabulary Crossword 1 Answer Key

Across
2. Clothing worn by military personnel
6. Ditch or channel
7. Tuft of hair that grows in a different direction
9. Pulled or drawn tight
11. Good condition or proper form
15. Stare wonderingly or stupidly
16. Direct; to the point
18. Charmingly odd
19. An interpretation
20. Substantiate by supplying evidence
21. Indispensable properties that characterize or identify
22. Reach about uncertainly or to feel one's way
23. Criticize

Down
1. Turned or placed at an angle
2. Something accidentally good or successful
3. Description of a place's terrain
4. People of a noble or wealthy class
5. Restlessly active or nervous
7. Group of trained personnel
8. Necessary; impossible to deter or evade
10. Appalling act, situation, or thing
12. Reserve; reluctance
13. Does not allow light to pass through
14. The order that makes things happen
15. Spinning device which maintains its orientation
16. Overwhelming, concentrated outpouring
17. Showing reverence

Things They Carried Vocabulary Crossword 2

Across
1. Moving or walking laboriously
2. Group of trained personnel
7. Good condition or proper form
8. Clothing worn by military personnel
10. An interpretation
11. Pulled or drawn tight
12. Spinning device which maintains its orientation
16. Disappear; vanish
20. Regard in an impersonal way
21. Tuft of hair that grows in a different direction
22. Easily understood; intelligible
23. Rudimentary communal toilet used in a camp or barracks

Down
1. Penetrating beyond what is superficial or obvious
2. Quality of being perfectly clear
3. Ditch or channel
4. Overwhelming, concentrated outpouring
5. Appalling act, situation, or thing
6. Criticize
9. People of a noble or wealthy class
12. Stare wonderingly or stupidly
13. Does not allow light to pass through
14. Permission
15. Unoriginal remark
17. Power of choosing; the will
18. Substantiate by supplying evidence
19. Displaying reverence or piety

Things They Carried Vocabulary Crossword 2 Answer Key

Across
1. Moving or walking laboriously
2. Group of trained personnel
7. Good condition or proper form
8. Clothing worn by military personnel
10. An interpretation
11. Pulled or drawn tight
12. Spinning device which maintains its orientation
16. Disappear; vanish
20. Regard in an impersonal way
21. Tuft of hair that grows in a different direction
22. Easily understood; intelligible
23. Rudimentary communal toilet used in a camp or barracks

Down
1. Penetrating beyond what is superficial or obvious
2. Quality of being perfectly clear
3. Ditch or channel
4. Overwhelming, concentrated outpouring
5. Appalling act, situation, or thing
6. Criticize
9. People of a noble or wealthy class
12. Stare wonderingly or stupidly
13. Does not allow light to pass through
14. Permission
15. Unoriginal remark
17. Power of choosing; the will
18. Substantiate by supplying evidence
19. Displaying reverence or piety

# Things They Carried Vocabulary Crossword 3

**Across**
1. Buddhist tower erected as a monument or shrine
3. Direct; to the point
4. Reach about uncertainly or to feel one's way
7. Camped in a temporary encampment, often in an unsheltered area
10. Grand; large
11. Rudimentary communal toilet used in a camp or barracks
13. One who does not believe an idea
14. An interpretation
16. Stare wonderingly or stupidly
18. Showing reverence
19. Village
20. Arousing sexual desire

**Down**
1. Penetrating beyond what is superficial or obvious
2. Displaying reverence or piety
3. Openly obvious
5. Military equipment such as ammunition
6. Indispensable properties that characterize or identify
7. Noisy uproar and confusion
8. Disemboweled; guts removed
9. Liquidating (a debt, such as a mortgage)
12. Reserve; reluctance
13. Restlessly active or nervous
14. Cleaning rod or stick with fabric at the end
15. Relationship with mutual trust or caring
17. State of being balanced

Things They Carried Vocabulary Crossword 3 Answer Key

Across
1. Buddhist tower erected as a monument or shrine
3. Direct; to the point
4. Reach about uncertainly or to feel one's way
7. Camped in a temporary encampment, often in an unsheltered area
10. Grand; large
11. Rudimentary communal toilet used in a camp or barracks
13. One who does not believe an idea
14. An interpretation
16. Stare wonderingly or stupidly
18. Showing reverence
19. Village
20. Arousing sexual desire

Down
1. Penetrating beyond what is superficial or obvious
2. Displaying reverence or piety
3. Openly obvious
5. Military equipment such as ammunition
6. Indispensable properties that characterize or identify
7. Noisy uproar and confusion
8. Disemboweled; guts removed
9. Liquidating (a debt, such as a mortgage)
12. Reserve; reluctance
13. Restlessly active or nervous
14. Cleaning rod or stick with fabric at the end
15. Relationship with mutual trust or caring
17. State of being balanced

Things They Carried Vocabulary Crossword 4

Across
1. Noisy uproar and confusion
2. Does not allow light to pass through
5. Showing reverence
7. Decay of tissue due to disease or infection
9. Reach about uncertainly or to feel one's way
10. Guessing based on facts; conclusion or opinion reached by conjecture
13. Group of trained personnel
15. Good condition or proper form
16. Description of a place's terrain
18. State of being balanced
19. Grand; large
20. Something accidentally good or successful
21. Rudimentary communal toilet used in a camp or barracks

Down
1. Direct; to the point
3. Penetrating beyond what is superficial or obvious
4. Disemboweled; guts removed
6. Turned or placed at an angle
7. Stare wonderingly or stupidly
8. Arousing sexual desire
9. People of a noble or wealthy class
10. Restlessly active or nervous
11. Harmony; agreement of interests or feeling
12. Overwhelming, concentrated outpouring
14. Basic monetary unit of South Vietnam
17. Buddhist tower erected as a monument or shrine

Things They Carried Vocabulary Crossword 4 Answer Key

Across
1. Noisy uproar and confusion
2. Does not allow light to pass through
5. Showing reverence
7. Decay of tissue due to disease or infection
9. Reach about uncertainly or to feel one's way
10. Guessing based on facts; conclusion or opinion reached by conjecture
13. Group of trained personnel
15. Good condition or proper form
16. Description of a place's terrain
18. State of being balanced
19. Grand; large
20. Something accidentally good or successful
21. Rudimentary communal toilet used in a camp or barracks

Down
1. Direct; to the point
3. Penetrating beyond what is superficial or obvious
4. Disemboweled; guts removed
6. Turned or placed at an angle
7. Stare wonderingly or stupidly
8. Arousing sexual desire
9. People of a noble or wealthy class
10. Restlessly active or nervous
11. Harmony; agreement of interests or feeling
12. Overwhelming, concentrated outpouring
14. Basic monetary unit of South Vietnam
17. Buddhist tower erected as a monument or shrine

Things They Carried Vocabulary Juggle Letters 1

1. TDATELUIP = 1. _____
   Unoriginal remark

2. GAZIIMORTN = 2. _____
   Liquidating (a debt, such as a mortgage)

3. KEID = 3. _____
   Ditch or channel

4. SFCLEK = 4. _____
   Small bits

5. UMHSBA = 5. _____
   Sudden attack made from a concealed position

6. DARONCNE = 6. _____
   Military equipment such as ammunition

7. OPPTRAR = 7. _____
   Relationship with mutual trust or caring

8. LHAMET = 8. _____
   Village

9. CSNRATTULNE = 9. _____
   Partially see-through

10. NTIQAU = 10. _____
    Charmingly odd

11. DBAMEL = 11. _____
    Noisy uproar and confusion

12. BGAEARR = 12. _____
    Overwhelming, concentrated outpouring

13. SGOYREOCP = 13. _____
    Spinning device which maintains its orientation

14. YRFUPEF = 14. _____
    Flattering, often exaggerated praise and publicity

Things They Carried Vocabulary Juggle Letters 1 Answer Key

1. TDATELUIP = 1. PLATITUDE
Unoriginal remark

2. GAZIIMORTN = 2. AMORTIZING
Liquidating (a debt, such as a mortgage)

3. KEID = 3. DIKE
Ditch or channel

4. SFCLEK = 4. FLECKS
Small bits

5. UMHSBA = 5. AMBUSH
Sudden attack made from a concealed position

6. DARONCNE = 6. ORDNANCE
Military equipment such as ammunition

7. OPPTRAR = 7. RAPPORT
Relationship with mutual trust or caring

8. LHAMET = 8. HAMLET
Village

9. CSNRATTULNE = 9. TRANSLUCENT
Partially see-through

10. NTIQAU =10. QUAINT
Charmingly odd

11. DBAMEL =11. BEDLAM
Noisy uproar and confusion

12. BGAEARR =12. BARRAGE
Overwhelming, concentrated outpouring

13. SGOYREOCP =13. GYROSCOPE
Spinning device which maintains its orientation

14. YRFUPEF =14. PUFFERY
Flattering, often exaggerated praise and publicity

Things They Carried Vocabulary Juggle Letters 2

1. BWSSA = 1. _____
Cleaning rod or stick with fabric at the end

2. PEAILLMBCA = 2. _____
Impossible to please or appease

3. LTUNB = 3. _____
Direct; to the point

4. TNCLOSUPIEA = 4. _____
Guessing based on facts; conclusion or opinion reached by conjecture

5. NAGIMIROZT = 5. _____
Liquidating (a debt, such as a mortgage)

6. ULVRAG = 6. _____
Indecent

7. ONCPHTEHOSPRSE = 7. _____
Glowing

8. YDYTENSER = 8. _____
Inflammatory disorder of the lower intestinal tract

9. AAYUCESW = 9. _____
Raised roadway, as across water or marshland

10. UOVCH = 10. _____
Substantiate by supplying evidence

11. KUFEL = 11. _____
Something accidentally good or successful

12. LTTBAAN = 12. _____
Openly obvious

13. TERRPAU = 13. _____
State of being transported by a lofty emotion; ecstasy

14. VBLELAERINNU = 14. _____
Impossible to damage, injure, or wound

Things They Carried Vocabulary Juggle Letters 2 Answer Key

1. BWSSA = 1. SWABS
Cleaning rod or stick with fabric at the end

2. PEAILLMBCA = 2. IMPLACABLE
Impossible to please or appease

3. LTUNB = 3. BLUNT
Direct; to the point

4. TNCLOSUPIEA = 4. SPECULATION
Guessing based on facts; conclusion or opinion reached by conjecture

5. NAGIMIROZT = 5. AMORTIZING
Liquidating (a debt, such as a mortgage)

6. ULVRAG = 6. VULGAR
Indecent

7. ONCPHTEHOSPRSE = 7. PHOSPHORESCENT
Glowing

8. YDYTENSER = 8. DYSENTERY
Inflammatory disorder of the lower intestinal tract

9. AAYUCESW = 9. CAUSEWAY
Raised roadway, as across water or marshland

10. UOVCH = 10. VOUCH
Substantiate by supplying evidence

11. KUFEL = 11. FLUKE
Something accidentally good or successful

12. LTTBAAN = 12. BLATANT
Openly obvious

13. TERRPAU = 13. RAPTURE
State of being transported by a lofty emotion; ecstasy

14. VBLELAERINNU = 14. INVULNERABLE
Impossible to damage, injure, or wound

Things They Carried Vocabulary Juggle Letters 3

1. REUNCUNDEMEB = 1. _____
   Not carrying a burden

2. ERTSIPA = 2. _____
   Basic monetary unit of South Vietnam

3. VTIEMIREAP = 3. _____
   Necessary; impossible to deter or evade

4. EGPRCSOYO = 4. _____
   Spinning device which maintains its orientation

5. REPAUTR = 5. _____
   State of being transported by a lofty emotion; ecstasy

6. IESOP = 6. _____
   State of being balanced

7. RLBEAINOD = 7. _____
   Pocketed belt for holding ammunition

8. ROCIET = 8. _____
   Arousing sexual desire

9. DOGLNDIP = 9. _____
   Moving or walking laboriously

10. OTGARIMIZN = 10. _____
    Liquidating (a debt, such as a mortgage)

11. PGEA = 11. _____
    Stare wonderingly or stupidly

12. RNGEYT = 12. _____
    People of a noble or wealthy class

13. MBHASU = 13. _____
    Sudden attack made from a concealed position

14. TVITELAE = 14. _____
    Rise in the air and float

Things They Carried Vocabulary Juggle Letters 3 Answer Key

1. REUNCUNDEMEB = 1. UNENCUMBERED
   Not carrying a burden
2. ERTSIPA = 2. PIASTER
   Basic monetary unit of South Vietnam
3. VTIEMIREAP = 3. IMPERATIVE
   Necessary; impossible to deter or evade
4. EGPRCSOYO = 4. GYROSCOPE
   Spinning device which maintains its orientation
5. REPAUTR = 5. RAPTURE
   State of being transported by a lofty emotion; ecstasy
6. IESOP = 6. POISE
   State of being balanced
7. RLBEAINOD = 7. BANDOLIER
   Pocketed belt for holding ammunition
8. ROCIET = 8. EROTIC
   Arousing sexual desire
9. DOGLNDIP = 9. PLODDING
   Moving or walking laboriously
10. OTGARIMIZN =10. AMORTIZING
    Liquidating (a debt, such as a mortgage)
11. PGEA =11. GAPE
    Stare wonderingly or stupidly
12. RNGEYT =12. GENTRY
    People of a noble or wealthy class
13. MBHASU =13. AMBUSH
    Sudden attack made from a concealed position
14. TVITELAE =14. LEVITATE
    Rise in the air and float

Things They Carried Vocabulary Juggle Letters 4

1. FOONPUDR = 1. _____
   Penetrating beyond what is superficial or obvious

2. UVODET = 2. _____
   Displaying reverence or piety

3. TNRYEG = 3. _____
   People of a noble or wealthy class

4. SMAHBU = 4. _____
   Sudden attack made from a concealed position

5. SENECSE = 5. _____
   Indispensable properties that characterize or identify

6. SIEHTECTA = 6. _____
   Concerning the appreciation of beauty or good taste

7. RLEITK = 7. _____
   Good condition or proper form

8. LNTBU = 8. _____
   Direct; to the point

9. IVIDEFNTIE = 9. _____
   Certain or conclusive

10. SIUAGFET =10. _____
    Clothing worn by military personnel

11. MAIETVEPRI =11. _____
    Necessary; impossible to deter or evade

12. TIKSPCE =12. _____
    One who does not believe an idea

13. IKLOWCC =13. _____
    Tuft of hair that grows in a different direction

14. BNLATEGI =14. _____
    Real or concrete

Things They Carried Vocabulary Juggle Letters 4 Answer Key

1. FOONPUDR = 1. PROFOUND
Penetrating beyond what is superficial or obvious

2. UVODET = 2. DEVOUT
Displaying reverence or piety

3. TNRYEG = 3. GENTRY
People of a noble or wealthy class

4. SMAHBU = 4. AMBUSH
Sudden attack made from a concealed position

5. SENECSE = 5. ESSENCE
Indispensable properties that characterize or identify

6. SIEHTECTA = 6. AESTHETIC
Concerning the appreciation of beauty or good taste

7. RLEITK = 7. KILTER
Good condition or proper form

8. LNTBU = 8. BLUNT
Direct; to the point

9. IVIDEFNTIE = 9. DEFINITIVE
Certain or conclusive

10. SIUAGFET =10. FATIGUES
Clothing worn by military personnel

11. MAIETVEPRI =11. IMPERATIVE
Necessary; impossible to deter or evade

12. TIKSPCE =12. SKEPTIC
One who does not believe an idea

13. IKLOWCC =13. COWLICK
Tuft of hair that grows in a different direction

14. BNLATEGI =14. TANGIBLE
Real or concrete

| | |
|---|---|
| ACQUIESCENCE | Consent by giving in |
| AESTHETIC | Concerning the appreciation of beauty or good taste |
| AFFLUENT | Wealthy |
| AMBUSH | Sudden attack made from a concealed position |
| AMORTIZING | Liquidating (a debt, such as a mortgage) |

| | |
|---|---|
| ATROCITY | Appalling act, situation, or thing |
| BANDOLIER | Pocketed belt for holding ammunition |
| BARRAGE | Overwhelming, concentrated outpouring |
| BEDLAM | Noisy uproar and confusion |
| BIVOUACKED | Camped in a temporary encampment, often in an unsheltered area |

| | |
|---|---|
| BLATANT | Openly obvious |
| BLUNT | Direct; to the point |
| CADRE | Group of trained personnel |
| CATHARSIS | Purifying or figurative cleansing of the emotions |
| CAUSATION | The order that makes things happen |

| | |
|---|---|
| CAUSEWAY | Raised roadway, as across water or marshland |
| CENSURE | Criticize |
| CLARITY | Quality of being perfectly clear |
| CLEARANCE | Permission |
| COMPLICITY | Participation in a crime or wrongdoing |

| COMPOSURE | Quality of being calm and even-tempered |
|---|---|
| CONCORD | Harmony; agreement of interests or feeling |
| CONVICTIONS | Beliefs; morals; values |
| COORDINATES | Directions for a location relating to longitude and latitude |
| COWLICK | Tuft of hair that grows in a different direction |

| | |
|---|---|
| DEFINITIVE | Certain or conclusive |
| DEVOUT | Displaying reverence or piety |
| DIKE | Ditch or channel |
| DYSENTERY | Inflammatory disorder of the lower intestinal tract |
| EMBODIED | Represented in bodily or material form |

| | |
|---|---|
| EROTIC | Arousing sexual desire |
| ESSENCE | Indispensable properties that characterize or identify |
| EVAPORATE | Disappear; vanish |
| EVISCERATED | Disemboweled; guts removed |
| EXUBERANCE | Quality of being extravagantly joyful |

| | |
|---|---|
| FATIGUES | Clothing worn by military personnel |
| FLECKS | Small bits |
| FLUKE | Something accidentally good or successful |
| GANGRENE | Decay of tissue due to disease or infection |
| GAPE | Stare wonderingly or stupidly |

| | |
|---|---|
| GENTRY | People of a noble or wealthy class |
| GROPE | Reach about uncertainly or to feel one's way |
| GYROSCOPE | Spinning device which maintains its orientation |
| HAMLET | Village |
| IMMENSE | Grand; large |

|  |  |
|---|---|
| IMPERATIVE | Necessary; impossible to deter or evade |
| IMPLACABLE | Impossible to please or appease |
| INFATUATION | Foolish, unreasoning, or extravagant passion or attraction |
| INVULNERABLE | Impossible to damage, injure, or wound |
| KILTER | Good condition or proper form |

| | |
|---|---|
| LATRINE | Rudimentary communal toilet used in a camp or barracks |
| LAXITY | State of slack, negligence, or carelessness |
| LEVITATE | Rise in the air and float |
| LUCID | Easily understood; intelligible |
| MENACING | Threatening |

| | |
|---|---|
| MUNDANE | Ordinary; common |
| OBJECTIFY | Regard in an impersonal way |
| OPAQUE | Does not allow light to pass through |
| ORDNANCE | Military equipment such as ammunition |
| PAGODA | Buddhist tower erected as a monument or shrine |

| PHOSPHORESCENT | Glowing |
| --- | --- |
| PIASTER | Basic monetary unit of South Vietnam |
| PIOUS | Showing reverence |
| PLATITUDE | Unoriginal remark |
| PLODDING | Moving or walking laboriously |

| POISE | State of being balanced |
| --- | --- |
| PROFOUND | Penetrating beyond what is superficial or obvious |
| PUFFERY | Flattering, often exaggerated praise and publicity |
| QUAINT | Charmingly odd |
| RAPPORT | Relationship with mutual trust or caring |

| RAPTURE | State of being transported by a lofty emotion; ecstasy |
| --- | --- |
| RECTITUDE | Moral righteousness |
| REPROACHED | Charged oneself with blame or a mistake |
| RETICENCE | Reserve; reluctance |
| SKEPTIC | One who does not believe an idea |

| | |
|---|---|
| SKEWED | Turned or placed at an angle |
| SKITTISH | Restlessly active or nervous |
| SPECULATION | Guessing based on facts; conclusion or opinion reached by conjecture |
| SPIN | An interpretation |
| SUPERLATIVES | Things of the highest excellence |

|  |  |
|---|---|
| SWABS | Cleaning rod or stick with fabric at the end |
| TANGIBLE | Real or concrete |
| TAUT | Pulled or drawn tight |
| TOPOGRAPHY | Description of a place's terrain |
| TRANSLUCENT | Partially see-through |

| | |
|---|---|
| UNENCUMBERED | Not carrying a burden |
| VOLITION | Power of choosing; the will |
| VOUCH | Substantiate by supplying evidence |
| VULGAR | Indecent |

Things They Carried Vocab

| HAMLET | SPIN | QUAINT | BANDOLIER | MUNDANE |
|---|---|---|---|---|
| SUPERLATIVES | GROPE | TOPOGRAPHY | DYSENTERY | CATHARSIS |
| POISE | ATROCITY | FREE SPACE | IMPERATIVE | CENSURE |
| INFATUATION | LAXITY | VOUCH | COMPOSURE | RECTITUDE |
| LUCID | SPECULATION | RAPTURE | FLECKS | PAGODA |

Things They Carried Vocab

| SWABS | SKEPTIC | CAUSEWAY | PUFFERY | BIVOUACKED |
|---|---|---|---|---|
| CLARITY | SKEWED | TAUT | AESTHETIC | EROTIC |
| DIKE | LATRINE | FREE SPACE | EVAPORATE | GYROSCOPE |
| CADRE | RETICENCE | EMBODIED | AMORTIZING | GENTRY |
| VOLITION | EXUBERANCE | PHOSPHORESCENT | UNENCUMBERED | ORDNANCE |

Things They Carried Vocab

| SPECULATION | GAPE | IMPERATIVE | VULGAR | GANGRENE |
|---|---|---|---|---|
| RAPPORT | LAXITY | KILTER | REPROACHED | INFATUATION |
| AFFLUENT | RAPTURE | FREE SPACE | INVULNERABLE | EVISCERATED |
| FLUKE | EVAPORATE | IMMENSE | COWLICK | UNENCUMBERED |
| CAUSEWAY | SUPERLATIVES | TANGIBLE | PROFOUND | LUCID |

Things They Carried Vocab

| PAGODA | LATRINE | FLECKS | ORDNANCE | OBJECTIFY |
|---|---|---|---|---|
| ACQUIESCENCE | CONCORD | QUAINT | GROPE | HAMLET |
| SPIN | TOPOGRAPHY | FREE SPACE | EXUBERANCE | TAUT |
| CLEARANCE | DIKE | COMPLICITY | RETICENCE | BIVOUACKED |
| LEVITATE | BANDOLIER | CAUSATION | EMBODIED | VOLITION |

Things They Carried Vocab

| TOPOGRAPHY | LAXITY | INFATUATION | SPIN | BLUNT |
|---|---|---|---|---|
| PHOSPHORESCENT | EVISCERATED | TRANSLUCENT | EXUBERANCE | AMBUSH |
| VOLITION | VULGAR | FREE SPACE | QUAINT | ESSENCE |
| COMPLICITY | TANGIBLE | CAUSEWAY | IMPERATIVE | SPECULATION |
| BEDLAM | COORDINATES | RAPTURE | PIASTER | CENSURE |

Things They Carried Vocab

| BANDOLIER | LEVITATE | VOUCH | ORDNANCE | SKITTISH |
|---|---|---|---|---|
| RETICENCE | RECTITUDE | OBJECTIFY | IMMENSE | PLODDING |
| RAPPORT | BLATANT | FREE SPACE | CLEARANCE | BIVOUACKED |
| FLECKS | PROFOUND | EROTIC | CONVICTIONS | COMPOSURE |
| EMBODIED | SWABS | AMORTIZING | AFFLUENT | DIKE |

Things They Carried Vocab

| COMPLICITY | SPECULATION | EROTIC | INVULNERABLE | GYROSCOPE |
|---|---|---|---|---|
| LUCID | SKEPTIC | TOPOGRAPHY | BLATANT | SWABS |
| HAMLET | GAPE | FREE SPACE | BLUNT | PIOUS |
| CONVICTIONS | GANGRENE | BARRAGE | CAUSEWAY | PLODDING |
| OPAQUE | MUNDANE | DYSENTERY | BEDLAM | CADRE |

Things They Carried Vocab

| TAUT | UNENCUMBERED | FLUKE | BIVOUACKED | QUAINT |
|---|---|---|---|---|
| SKEWED | LATRINE | LAXITY | AESTHETIC | PIASTER |
| EVAPORATE | LEVITATE | FREE SPACE | COMPOSURE | TANGIBLE |
| AMORTIZING | MENACING | KILTER | EMBODIED | COORDINATES |
| PAGODA | ESSENCE | IMPERATIVE | ATROCITY | EXUBERANCE |

Things They Carried Vocab

| BARRAGE | PLODDING | PIASTER | QUAINT | COORDINATES |
|---|---|---|---|---|
| OPAQUE | POISE | BIVOUACKED | LATRINE | PROFOUND |
| SWABS | FLUKE | FREE SPACE | PLATITUDE | PIOUS |
| VOUCH | RECTITUDE | HAMLET | SKEWED | REPROACHED |
| TRANSLUCENT | MENACING | CAUSATION | ACQUIESCENCE | BEDLAM |

Things They Carried Vocab

| AFFLUENT | SPIN | VULGAR | PAGODA | GAPE |
|---|---|---|---|---|
| GROPE | IMPLACABLE | CLARITY | AMORTIZING | GANGRENE |
| MUNDANE | INVULNERABLE | FREE SPACE | EVAPORATE | IMPERATIVE |
| FATIGUES | COMPLICITY | RAPPORT | EMBODIED | FLECKS |
| GYROSCOPE | CONCORD | TAUT | CAUSEWAY | PHOSPHORESCENT |

Things They Carried Vocab

| GANGRENE | BANDOLIER | TANGIBLE | CATHARSIS | CADRE |
|---|---|---|---|---|
| AMORTIZING | SPECULATION | REPROACHED | EVISCERATED | POISE |
| SKITTISH | GAPE | FREE SPACE | COORDINATES | VOUCH |
| MUNDANE | SUPERLATIVES | LUCID | GYROSCOPE | EMBODIED |
| DYSENTERY | FLUKE | COMPOSURE | EROTIC | CONCORD |

Things They Carried Vocab

| TAUT | PIOUS | BARRAGE | PHOSPHORESCENT | INVULNERABLE |
|---|---|---|---|---|
| CONVICTIONS | KILTER | PLATITUDE | CAUSEWAY | TRANSLUCENT |
| FATIGUES | PIASTER | FREE SPACE | LAXITY | AESTHETIC |
| COMPLICITY | QUAINT | RECTITUDE | IMMENSE | LEVITATE |
| BLATANT | LATRINE | RAPTURE | DIKE | BEDLAM |

Things They Carried Vocab

| ORDNANCE | POISE | HAMLET | IMPLACABLE | EROTIC |
|---|---|---|---|---|
| RETICENCE | COORDINATES | COMPLICITY | FLUKE | LATRINE |
| DIKE | GANGRENE | FREE SPACE | PIOUS | PROFOUND |
| FLECKS | MENACING | RECTITUDE | EVISCERATED | AMORTIZING |
| CLEARANCE | CATHARSIS | LUCID | TANGIBLE | GENTRY |

Things They Carried Vocab

| VULGAR | UNENCUMBERED | ESSENCE | SKEPTIC | BANDOLIER |
|---|---|---|---|---|
| CADRE | GAPE | RAPTURE | LAXITY | TOPOGRAPHY |
| TAUT | BLATANT | FREE SPACE | VOUCH | SKEWED |
| EXUBERANCE | GYROSCOPE | LEVITATE | GROPE | REPROACHED |
| PUFFERY | RAPPORT | SWABS | PAGODA | CAUSATION |

Things They Carried Vocab

| CONVICTIONS | KILTER | RAPTURE | IMPLACABLE | CATHARSIS |
|---|---|---|---|---|
| AESTHETIC | DEVOUT | PHOSPHORESCENT | VOLITION | CLARITY |
| TANGIBLE | LEVITATE | FREE SPACE | SPIN | RECTITUDE |
| EVAPORATE | GENTRY | RAPPORT | QUAINT | PLODDING |
| BARRAGE | BLUNT | DYSENTERY | TAUT | PIASTER |

Things They Carried Vocab

| FLECKS | AMBUSH | BANDOLIER | INFATUATION | EROTIC |
|---|---|---|---|---|
| VOUCH | SKEWED | SKEPTIC | COMPOSURE | AMORTIZING |
| CAUSATION | CONCORD | FREE SPACE | GANGRENE | SWABS |
| LAXITY | FATIGUES | BEDLAM | SKITTISH | OBJECTIFY |
| GAPE | COORDINATES | PIOUS | TRANSLUCENT | CLEARANCE |

Things They Carried Vocab

| TOPOGRAPHY | SPECULATION | BLUNT | QUAINT | OPAQUE |
|---|---|---|---|---|
| RAPPORT | TANGIBLE | FLUKE | PUFFERY | VOLITION |
| AESTHETIC | PHOSPHORESCENT | FREE SPACE | SUPERLATIVES | GROPE |
| SWABS | PIOUS | CONVICTIONS | RAPTURE | COMPOSURE |
| AMBUSH | INVULNERABLE | GAPE | POISE | VOUCH |

Things They Carried Vocab

| EXUBERANCE | CAUSATION | AFFLUENT | GYROSCOPE | DEVOUT |
|---|---|---|---|---|
| RETICENCE | LATRINE | CLARITY | ESSENCE | AMORTIZING |
| SKEWED | CONCORD | FREE SPACE | EVISCERATED | EMBODIED |
| INFATUATION | CAUSEWAY | PIASTER | PLODDING | LEVITATE |
| PLATITUDE | CENSURE | SKEPTIC | TRANSLUCENT | IMPERATIVE |

Things They Carried Vocab

| MENACING | SKEWED | FLECKS | FLUKE | PLODDING |
|---|---|---|---|---|
| COMPLICITY | GANGRENE | BANDOLIER | PUFFERY | LEVITATE |
| AMORTIZING | IMMENSE | FREE SPACE | CLEARANCE | RETICENCE |
| COORDINATES | INFATUATION | RECTITUDE | HAMLET | DYSENTERY |
| COMPOSURE | OPAQUE | GAPE | COWLICK | BARRAGE |

Things They Carried Vocab

| SPIN | SPECULATION | PROFOUND | RAPTURE | BLATANT |
|---|---|---|---|---|
| IMPERATIVE | PHOSPHORESCENT | PIOUS | PAGODA | PLATITUDE |
| FATIGUES | EMBODIED | FREE SPACE | CAUSATION | REPROACHED |
| ESSENCE | RAPPORT | TANGIBLE | LUCID | LATRINE |
| SKEPTIC | ORDNANCE | ATROCITY | CAUSEWAY | MUNDANE |

Things They Carried Vocab

| BLATANT | SKEWED | DEVOUT | PLODDING | GROPE |
|---|---|---|---|---|
| CONVICTIONS | COWLICK | TRANSLUCENT | ACQUIESCENCE | RECTITUDE |
| PIASTER | SKITTISH | FREE SPACE | AESTHETIC | EVISCERATED |
| AMBUSH | SKEPTIC | FLECKS | CLARITY | INFATUATION |
| SPECULATION | VULGAR | CONCORD | SWABS | ESSENCE |

Things They Carried Vocab

| ATROCITY | EROTIC | OPAQUE | COORDINATES | OBJECTIFY |
|---|---|---|---|---|
| MENACING | RAPTURE | PAGODA | LEVITATE | LATRINE |
| BARRAGE | GYROSCOPE | FREE SPACE | QUAINT | PROFOUND |
| GENTRY | PHOSPHORESCENT | TANGIBLE | HAMLET | DIKE |
| BANDOLIER | CATHARSIS | PUFFERY | FATIGUES | AMORTIZING |

## Things They Carried Vocab

| EVAPORATE | DEVOUT | COWLICK | DYSENTERY | OBJECTIFY |
|---|---|---|---|---|
| GENTRY | GROPE | INVULNERABLE | PLODDING | TAUT |
| UNENCUMBERED | PIASTER | FREE SPACE | ACQUIESCENCE | INFATUATION |
| BANDOLIER | BLUNT | SWABS | SKITTISH | AESTHETIC |
| IMMENSE | GAPE | IMPERATIVE | DIKE | LUCID |

## Things They Carried Vocab

| RAPPORT | BEDLAM | VOUCH | KILTER | GYROSCOPE |
|---|---|---|---|---|
| PLATITUDE | VULGAR | EROTIC | DEFINITIVE | CAUSATION |
| PIOUS | CATHARSIS | FREE SPACE | SPECULATION | CENSURE |
| SPIN | IMPLACABLE | ORDNANCE | AMBUSH | RECTITUDE |
| COMPLICITY | BLATANT | SKEPTIC | CLEARANCE | BIVOUACKED |

Things They Carried Vocab

| IMPLACABLE | UNENCUMBERED | AFFLUENT | REPROACHED | CADRE |
|---|---|---|---|---|
| GROPE | FATIGUES | ESSENCE | RAPTURE | BLUNT |
| PUFFERY | COORDINATES | FREE SPACE | SKITTISH | RETICENCE |
| SUPERLATIVES | COWLICK | LEVITATE | PLATITUDE | CONCORD |
| IMMENSE | CLARITY | SPIN | BARRAGE | FLUKE |

Things They Carried Vocab

| EROTIC | GYROSCOPE | CENSURE | TRANSLUCENT | PHOSPHORESCENT |
|---|---|---|---|---|
| COMPLICITY | CLEARANCE | PROFOUND | AMBUSH | EVISCERATED |
| CAUSATION | QUAINT | FREE SPACE | CONVICTIONS | CAUSEWAY |
| MENACING | FLECKS | KILTER | SPECULATION | INVULNERABLE |
| BIVOUACKED | ATROCITY | OPAQUE | PIOUS | CATHARSIS |

Things They Carried Vocab

| LATRINE | CAUSATION | SKEPTIC | COORDINATES | GANGRENE |
|---|---|---|---|---|
| TRANSLUCENT | CADRE | EVISCERATED | GAPE | FLUKE |
| FLECKS | VOUCH | FREE SPACE | KILTER | COWLICK |
| TOPOGRAPHY | AMORTIZING | MUNDANE | PIASTER | MENACING |
| INVULNERABLE | ATROCITY | LEVITATE | DIKE | PIOUS |

Things They Carried Vocab

| DYSENTERY | EVAPORATE | CLARITY | CLEARANCE | PUFFERY |
|---|---|---|---|---|
| PHOSPHORESCENT | AESTHETIC | GYROSCOPE | SPECULATION | RAPPORT |
| CAUSEWAY | PLODDING | FREE SPACE | IMPERATIVE | VOLITION |
| SKITTISH | AFFLUENT | BARRAGE | VULGAR | REPROACHED |
| POISE | COMPOSURE | BLUNT | SWABS | ESSENCE |

Things They Carried Vocab

| SWABS | PIOUS | BEDLAM | SPIN | OBJECTIFY |
|---|---|---|---|---|
| REPROACHED | BLUNT | GYROSCOPE | FLECKS | BARRAGE |
| EROTIC | FATIGUES | FREE SPACE | PLATITUDE | POISE |
| PHOSPHORESCENT | CADRE | LEVITATE | PAGODA | LAXITY |
| AMBUSH | ATROCITY | ACQUIESCENCE | SKEWED | CAUSATION |

Things They Carried Vocab

| PIASTER | TOPOGRAPHY | KILTER | RECTITUDE | DEVOUT |
|---|---|---|---|---|
| MUNDANE | PLODDING | OPAQUE | IMMENSE | ESSENCE |
| BANDOLIER | COMPLICITY | FREE SPACE | LATRINE | CLARITY |
| TAUT | PUFFERY | INVULNERABLE | RAPPORT | SPECULATION |
| VULGAR | INFATUATION | HAMLET | COORDINATES | COWLICK |

Things They Carried Vocab

| COMPOSURE | ATROCITY | INVULNERABLE | GENTRY | PIASTER |
|---|---|---|---|---|
| FLECKS | EVISCERATED | PLODDING | SPIN | CATHARSIS |
| BARRAGE | BLUNT | FREE SPACE | AMORTIZING | CONCORD |
| EROTIC | BIVOUACKED | INFATUATION | VOLITION | VOUCH |
| HAMLET | DEFINITIVE | PLATITUDE | COMPLICITY | EXUBERANCE |

Things They Carried Vocab

| BANDOLIER | QUAINT | COWLICK | IMPERATIVE | PHOSPHORESCENT |
|---|---|---|---|---|
| TOPOGRAPHY | TANGIBLE | ACQUIESCENCE | TRANSLUCENT | FATIGUES |
| COORDINATES | ORDNANCE | FREE SPACE | BLATANT | BEDLAM |
| SPECULATION | FLUKE | PROFOUND | LAXITY | PIOUS |
| GYROSCOPE | LATRINE | RETICENCE | LUCID | MUNDANE |